M000311921

# REVIEWS

"One of the most striking features of this book is the level of discomfort and raw truth you will experience within these pages. We, women know, and yet many of us remain silent! This book is both a challenge and manifesto for women everywhere, to embrace their true selves, own their imperfections and reclaim their feminine power.

It doesn't claim to have all the answers, but it does ask us to look inside and make the choice and dare to be brave-brave enough to NOT allow ourselves to be forced in to conformity and caricatures of who we are as both women and humans.

We are human but our power lies in embracing our own feminine energies, recognizing that while it is different than the masculine force, it is in no way inferior or lacking in it's power to effect change. It's different, it's powerful, and it's Divine!" - Tonye Tariah, www.freedomatthecrossroads.com

# UNLEASHING
# HER WILD

**Freeing Feminine Instinct and Intuition as Guides
to an Awakened Life**

Unleashing Her Wild: Freeing Feminine Instinct and Intuition as Guides to an Awakened Life
2019 Golden Brick Road Publishing House Inc. Trade Paperback Edition
Copyright © 2019 Golden Brick Road Publishing House

All Rights Reserved. No part of this book can be scanned, distributed or copied without permission. This book or any portion thereof may not be reproduced or used in any manner whatsoever without the express written permission of the publisher at kylee@gbrph.ca - except for the use of brief quotations in a book review. The author has independently contributed to the content of this book, irrespective of the other author's contribution, viewpoint or advice.

The authors each own the copyright of their original work within their chapter and have made every effort to ensure the accuracy of the information within this book was correct at time of publication. The authors do not assume and hereby disclaim any liability to any party for any loss, damage, or disruption caused by errors or omissions, whether such errors or omissions result from accident, negligence, or any other cause. This book is not intended to be a substitute for the medical advice of a licensed physician. The reader should consult with their doctor in any matters relating to his / her health.

Every effort has been made to trace copyright holders and to obtain their permission for the use of copyright material. The publisher apologizes for any errors or omissions in the above list and would be grateful if notified of any corrections that should be incorporated in future reprints or editions of this book.

The publisher is not responsible for websites (or their content) that are not owned by the publisher.

Published in Canada, for Global Distribution by Golden Brick Road Publishing House Inc.

www.goldenbrickroad.pub
For more information email: kylee@gbrph.ca

ISBN:
Paperback: 978-1-988736-70-9
Ebook: 978-1-988736-84-6
Kindle: 978-1-988736-85-3

To order additional copies of this book: orders@gbrph.ca

# UNLEASHING HER WILD

### Freeing Feminine Instinct and Intuition as Guides to an Awakened Life

**By:** Donna Tack, Kiki Carr, Renee Kaylor, Danielle Laura, Eleni Grey, Heather Allison, Mollie Lyddane, Michelle Arnold, S.C. Vollmer, Angelica Grace

# CONTENTS

# PREFACE

Unleashing *Her Wild* colors outside the lines, it unleashes a creative, poetic, loving, and fierce story of the wild woman and Feminine energy that is within all of us. The evolution of a woman during one lifetime is vast; our authors want women and the Feminine within all of us to remember that, to allow life to be infinite.

In our true nature, we create. We create life and every moment within it. We envision our future and decide how we experience our existence leading up to it. Do we see beauty and opportunities for discovery, or do we see pain and despair? Have we become numb, preventing us from designing and manifesting anything at all, closed off and left to see and feel . . . nothing?

We are wise beyond our years, we remember what she before us experienced. Society wants us to forget, punishes us, chains us . . . to be quiet, inward, and submissive.

What would it be like to be unleashed?

This book remembers and shares experiences of feeling limited and urging the resistance, going against the grain and tapping into intuition. Acting on, following a sense, without ego or external pressures. Allowing Feminine instinct to BE one with the moment, without influence, and make her choice as she knows to be truth. To feel as one, to feel whole, in our self.

On a continuous journey, we unwrap a part of our self in each moment. Grateful for the new found solitude, strength, and self assurance. With each experience we are *Unleashing Her Wild*.

# INTRODUCTION

Happiness in life is achieved through balance. When we hear this, our social conditioning may immediately visualizes stability between family and career, but the balance we each need is deeper than that. A reflex to immediately look at our external world comes from the Masculine energy within all of us. Everything in the Universe is governed by both Masculine and Feminine energies; our emotions, our health, our surrounding environment: Feng Shui. What is the cause of our uncertainty? Our chaos? What is inside of us that is manifesting tension?

Why do we feel pulled in different directions?

All people all born with both Yin and Yang energies, our universal energies. They are commonly referred to as Divine Feminine (yin) and Divine Masculine (yang). This is not in reference to social structures or gender roles of male and female. We all have both energies within us. Some people lean more to a greater or lesser Yin, or greater or lesser Yang. Neither Yin or Yang are absolute, and we can be influenced in our environment to sway greater towards one over the other. Awakening our wild Divine Feminine in our society, within this lifetime, helps us to find a sort of balance.

Our society has encouraged greater Yang for centuries. This is strong, heightened Masculine energy. Greater Yang energy is assertive, goal-oriented, accomplished, and dominant. This energy is associated with daytime, activity, vision, and power. While some of Yin's traits are: calm, internal, intuition, quiet, receptive, and softness, Yin is also the negative charge representing: closed in spaces, cold, discreet, indirect, and storage. While both Yin and Yang traits can be seen as welcomed characteristics when needed, too much of anything can be overbearing and unbalanced.

We have been taught to separate the energies, to distinguish the two. Masculine as strong, Feminine as weak. Yet, . . . [t]he two opposites of Yin and Yang attract and complement each other and, as their symbol illustrates, each side has at its core an element of the other (represented by the small dots). Neither pole is superior to the other and, as an increase in one brings a corresponding decrease in the other, a correct balance between the two poles must be reached in order to achieve harmony. In Chinese mythology Yin and Yang were born from chaos when the Universe was first created.[1]

By *Unleashing Her Wild*, freeing the Feminine energy and following instinct and intuition as guides, we will live a more awakened human experience. We can shape our environment to a harmonic one. This book will share stories of women unleashing her wild Feminine in various life situations through acceptance, confidence, and sexuality, and by remembering and starting to reconcile with memories passed down from her ancestors.

---

1    Cartwright, M. (2018, May 16). Yin and Yang. *Ancient History Encyclopedia.* Retrieved from https://www.ancient.eu/Yin_and_Yang/

SOME DAYS I AM MORE WOLF THAN WOMAN, AND I AM STILL LEARNING HOW TO STOP APOLOGIZING FOR MY WILD.

- Nikita Gill

UNLEASHING HER WILD

WE ALL
POSSESS
BOTH
FEMININE

# AND
# MASCULINE
# ENERGIES

UNLEASHING HER WILD

# CHAPTER 01

# THE REMEMBERING

## BY: DONNA TACK

*"My beautiful sisters, of course you must shine; you are made of the stars."*

# DONNA TACK

~~~~~~~~~~~~~~~~

ig: @nightskydw | fb: @nightskydivinewellness

Donna Tack is the owner of Night Sky Divine Wellness, a Reiki and energy healing practice. *"Reclaim Your Divinity"* is her company catchphrase, and she is passionate about helping people do just that. Donna holds a strong belief that we are all on a beautiful, sometimes painful, and glorious journey back to our Divine selves. Donna holds a certificate in counseling from Vancouver Community College. She has been in recovery from drugs and alcohol since 2009 and has dedicated her life to helping women find recovery from trauma and addictions.

She has a published short story in *Lessons from my Child*, in which she shares her journey as the mother of a terminally disabled child. Donna's son passed over to the spirit world in 2013. This opened a door to her pursuit of death doula work so that she can help others process their grief. She is pursuing certification in this healing modality in 2019. Donna's reclamation of her indigenous background has helped her to reconnect with Mother Earth and the wild woman within her.

**M**y beautiful sisters, we are at war. We are at war with our-selves, our bodies, our too much-ness, our wants, our needs, and our desires. Just as heartbreaking, we are at war with each other. We judge, we criticize, and we compete as if there is not enough of anything for us all.

We have forgotten who we are. We have forsaken who we have always been. We have forgotten who we were created to be: life givers, knowledge keepers, and holders of the sacred Divine. We have forgotten our Wild Feminine.

Let the recollection begin. Let us ask:

*How* did we forget ourselves?

*When* did we become so disconnected from that place within us that knows?

*What* caused this spiritual amnesia?

*Where* did it all go wrong?

For me, the forgetting started when I was a very young girl. I was told that I was too loud, too round, too aggressive, too much of everything, and so I started denying and rejecting all that was me.

I dreamed of being someone, anyone else but me. I learned to be quiet. I silenced my too loud voice, I starved my body with di-ets, and I conformed to ideals that didn't suit me. The most heart-breaking of all, I silenced the voice within that told me I was beau-tiful and strong.

I did not find out about my indigenous bloodline until recently. I have since learned it came from my paternal grandfather's side of the family. My great-grandmother carried both Apache and Chickasaw blood. I may not have known about my indigenous ancestry, but my spirit knew, my heart and soul knew. To be honest, anyone who looked at me knew I had indigenous heritage. I was called names like "wagon burner," "squaw," and "chug." I felt deeply ashamed about my looks and features. I turned away from anything that made me different and I tried to lighten my hair and my skin.

My childhood was dark and painful, full of every kind of abuse imaginable, which made the process of forgetting myself easier. It is very difficult to shine when you are shadowed in the darkness of other peoples' dreams. I spent most of my life armored against life itself. I protected my Divine light with fake smiles, conformity, and accomplishments. Deep inside, I was asleep. The Divine Goddess in me was forgotten.

I know I am not the only one. On any given day, I peruse my social media and see the faces of my beautiful sisters, highlighted in pictures filtered beyond recognition. I see bodies altered by science and latex and unrelenting workouts and diets. The endless selfies and gym poses constantly overflow on my newsfeed. We post reams of spiritual memes with no substance or understanding of what they mean. We have tweezed, plucked, and waxed ourselves into oblivion.

It breaks my heart because in their forgetfulness, women cannot see how beautiful and magnificent they are. Under the filters and the makeup are the most beautiful women I have ever seen. I can see them with my wild eyes, and I see their perfection.

When did your forgetting start? Can you touch it? Can you go back and see the moment it happened? Or like me, was it a series of lies told to you of your unworthiness? All the things that were a part of your too muchness? Who told you those lies of your unworthiness? Of your too muchness? When did you forget your Divine Truth? Who stole your power?

Does it scare you to think of being fully, conscientiously aware and awake to the Wild Feminine in you, to truly own your birthright and your innate divine power? I know it scared me. It terrified me in fact, and in those most vulnerable moments of my humanness and in my desperate desire to be loved and accepted by this world and all of its people, it sometimes still does.

*What will people think of me? How will it feel to show them the true me, with no filters, no shell of plastic armor, to protect the places that have been stored away for so long? Isn't it easier to stay asleep to my magic, to continue hiding that which scares not only me but the world?*

Not that long ago, the wild women, the medicine keepers, and the healers were burned at the stake, vilified, hated and feared. In some places, they still are. Even today, so many of our sisters on this planet are someone's property, mutilated, silenced, and thrown away. In the West, we are so privileged, so oblivious to the pain of our sisters, that we "forget" at an even deeper level. We forget what it means to have the privilege to call this wild place in ourselves into being. Where we can talk about it openly and seek it out in the light. So, when I ask myself, "Can you do it? Can you?" The answer, my sisters, is Yes. YES! YES! We must. How can we not, when so many do not even have the choice?

"But how?" you ask. How does one remember her Wild, Divine Feminine in a world that hates her and undermines her at every turn? In a world of deadlines, soccer practices, and traffic jams? In a world that paints strong women as bitches, uses our bodies to sell every product imaginable, and in which #metoo is a thing? In a world that seems anything but wild? Why would we want to? My question to you again is, "How can you not?"

This book has called to you, which tells me that you feel the stirring within you. It shows me that you remember, in small, déjà vu moments and quiet whispers. You remember that you are made of stars and meant for so much more. It comes as small rememberings at first, a stirring in your blood. A pull to the moon on a dark night, knowing you have danced under it before, somewhere at some time. It comes as a yearning to be barefoot in the grass or to dance with wild abandon. It is the pull of the ocean and the sound of the waves that makes your blood churn and makes you long for the wind in your hair. There are these small moments when we feel it in our bones, and like the wind, they are gone too quickly. These doors are few and precious, and we cannot continue to slam them shut. We must open them wide and explore what is inside.

For me, my remembering started with following the path of my ancestors and finding the part of me that had been locked away for so long. I had hidden the native in me, disowning it as something dirty or bad. I knew I needed to reclaim that part of me and find the beauty in it. I attended sweat lodge (Inipi) ceremonies and learned about the women warriors who had come and gone before me. I immersed myself in learning and followed the teachings and the medicines of my elders: the beautiful natural ways of the First Nations people. These teachings have a deep respect and connection to the land, the animals, the plants, and the elements. I connected with nature in profound, ceremonial ways. I received my spirit name, Night Sky Woman, and I felt like I finally knew who I was. Sisters, find out who you come from — *the women whose blood you carry.*

As I started to follow the cycles of nature and the Moon, my yearning to connect to Maka Ina, our Earth Mother, stirred in me, and I started to remember. In our collective amnesia, we have forgotten the beauty in the dance of our bodies in concert with Grandmother Moon. And so, my remembering continued in the reclaiming of my body and the honoring of my gift: my power to create life.

I started reading books that called to my spirit. As I nurtured this calling inside me, this calling in of the Wild, the Universe aligned with me and sent me circles of women. These women were aligned with the same purpose and desire to reclaim their own divinity, and they reflected the forgotten Wild Feminine back to me. Slowly I started to remember more than I had forgotten.

As women, we are often called upon to be everything to everyone, and in that calling we forget to be anything to ourselves. We are yoked by the burdens of our own desire for equality. We cry to be equal, forgetting that we have never been equal. We have always been something else. We have always been more than, stronger than, wiser than we have ever dreamed possible. We have always been the healers, the wisdom keepers, the life givers, and the backbone of every family, every tribe, and every community. History has tried to erase us, and it has done a good job.

In my work to reclaim these lost parts of myself, I have at times grasped at those precious fleeting moments of knowing, with a desperation and neediness to find the answers. I continued seeking outside myself for answers that lay only within. I have struggled and fought with my shadows and my demons, thinking they needed to be vanquished before I could step into the light. I was wrong. They need to be explored and embraced. The wild women have always called upon familiars that reside in the dark: the wolf, the raven, the cat. We dance under the Moon and the stars, and we are not afraid of the shadows. We must remember the beauty in the dark. No star can shine without it.

Our wounds, the dark places that we protect and hide away from the world, are doorways into our divinity. I will remind you again, dear sisters, that these doors are few and they are precious. Yet somehow we want to keep them locked. We do not want to open what we have spent so much time keeping closed.

We all have the scars of living and being human, yet we hide them away. This is our greatest mistake. To really know yourself, to embrace the Wild Feminine in you, you must fling open those doors and let light into every corner. Welcome every scar, every wrinkle, every wound, for *this is our truth*. We both are our stories and are not. We are dark and we are light; we are everything in between. We are beautiful and flawed and so incredibly, painfully human. This is true for everyone. When you compare yourself to others or are jealous of the accomplishments and the outside perfection of another, ask yourself, "*Who* is feeling these things?" Is it the wounded child, the scared teenager, the overwhelmed mother and woman in you? Become the observer of these feelings. The truth lies somewhere between your thoughts and feelings.

The Wild Feminine is the champion of women. She will encourage and support her sisters, and she knows there is more than enough of everything to go around. Embrace your sisters, hold them up, cheer them on. Call to them in your dreams; they will come. Call your ancestors, call your grandmothers and great-grandmothers. They will come. They will help you to remember.

We are so afraid of letting people see the flawed, imperfect, beautiful us. We fight against aging as if it is some monster meant to be held off at all costs. We revere the movie star and the supermodel, and we send our elders to hide in the care home. We do not want to see what we are so afraid of becoming. We fight against ourselves until we are exhausted, and we wonder why we have no energy. The signs of a woman who has forgotten her Wild are: exhaustion, feeling overwhelmed, a lack of desire for pleasure and sex, a lack of vision and creativity . . . The list goes on. We are overworked and overwhelmed. We are so tired.

When is the last time you made love with abandon, without worrying about how you looked or smelled? When was the last time you felt true joy and the freedom of your wildness? Our ancestors, our great-great-grandmothers understood and lived by the cycles of nature. They knew inherently what was needed, and they did not hide behind armors made of plastic. We are all indigenous to some place. We all have a history, a story. Every nationality has ancestry.

Our grandmothers knew that aging was a gift of wisdom and certainty. It was a place where the petty concerns of what others think didn't matter. The Crone was revered and sought out for her wisdom, teaching, and stories. Now we kill the Crone, we hide her away. We despise her, with her wrinkled skin and gnarled hands. We put her in the closet with the other demons we do not want anyone to see. Our ancestors knew how to instinctively care for their young, their mates, and their tribe. They knew when to rest and when to fight. They knew who they were and they understood their power and their gifts. It is *we* who have forgotten.

So my beautiful sisters, *this* is how we remember. We unlock those doors we have held tightly closed for so long. We fling them open, and we invite any one who cares to look inside. We answer the call of the wild that comes in the longing to be near the ocean, the woods, the streams and rivers that have held our secrets for eternity. I urge you to listen to the yearnings of your soul, the call to be free. Surround yourself with other women seeking the Wild Feminine. Call on your ancestors and learn your story, your history. Share it, know it, tell it and pass it to your daughters. Abandon yourself to joy, to freedom, to wildness. Embrace your dark places and integrate all of the shadows into who you are. Find ways to love and honor your body, to revere and worship her and all the ways she supports you. Listen to your intuition. Trust that feeling in your gut, that whisper in your soul, that tug in your heart. We have forgotten that connection and we ignore what we know is true. Trust the feeling when it tells you to walk away from the friend, the job, the man. Trust your inner knowing. *This* is the remembering.

My beautiful sisters, of course you must shine; you are made of the stars.

*I see you, Gramma*
*Shining in the sky,*
*Full and round and full of light.*
*I feel your pull, calling me;*
*Calling to my Wild Self.*
\*\*\*\*\*

*Oh, how I yearn to run free and play and howl*
*under your gaze*
*The stirring in my blood feels like a memory*
\*\*\*\*\*

*But here I am*
*Full and round and full of light,*
*tethered to this earth.*
*We are the same,*
*Me and you.*
\*\*\*\*\*

*So I will stay here and shine,*
*and I will call to the other wild things.*
*Together we will dance*
*and run and howl in my dreams of you,*
*until I am free of this Earth and become one of*
*the stars that shimmer and shine by your side.*

JUST BE.

CHAPTER 02

# COLOR OUTSIDE THE LINE

BY: KIKI CARR

*"She found herself by reconnecting with who she used to be."*

# KIKI CARR

~~~~~~~~

ig: @carrkristine | fb: @carrkristine

www.kristinecarr.com

With a dreamer's mind and the soul of a wanderer, Kiki Carr (also known as Kristine), has been adventurous and ambitious since she was a young girl. As with most women, when the need to fit in and blend into a mold became a priority, she grew more and more disconnected to her true self. This found her in academia, in careers with titles, volunteering every ounce of herself, and always climbing mountains to please others. Undeniably passionate about her service to others, Kiki began a career in social services with goals to change the world to prove her worthiness amongst the crowd.

A quarter life crisis ensued. With a bachelor of arts degree majoring in criminology and justice and minors in domestic violence and policing, Kiki packed up her desk and left her job of seven years. Thus began a five year journey in rediscovering a life that would fulfill her, heal her from thirteen years of mental illness, and welcome back that ambitious little girl.

Kiki is a passionate writer and storyteller, encouraging sustainable goal-setting and self-care practices. She believes that we all have the ability to design, create, and curate the life that we want to live, a life that we love fully and completely.

## Wild Child

I was always told that *wild* meant unruly, unnatural, disorderly, and ultimately seen as negative. Now, for me, wild means being free. Free to be outside of the box. Free to explore.

Growing up, it was much safer to color inside the lines and stay inside a box that depicted the average lifestyle; exploring and doing things differently were met with discouragement. Be a child, grow up, go to school, go to postsecondary, get a job, get married, have kids, and watch the cycle start all over again. This was the box that I worked my whole life to be a part of. I did everything that I was supposed to. I was a soldier to monotony because I was guaranteed to be happy if I did so.

I grew up in a school system that taught me I needed to pass tests to have self-worth, even though those kinds of tests worked against my brain's natural rhythm. I learned from organized spirituality to fear and follow, not to explore, be curious, ask questions, and gain a deeper understanding. I was influenced by society to believe that, as a woman, I should cover up and feel shame about my body. The idea of being wild meant being out of order, and being feminine meant hiding and staying in line. The concepts of wild or feminine were not taught with power, tenacity, or vibrancy but rather the opposite.

Fear equaled love in all parts of my life, and being disciplined meant that I would be better. I became scared of everything and everyone, which turned into anxiety and depression. I kept being shoved inside this box and I wanted nothing more than to please everyone so I could be accepted and loved. I was waiting for that day to come when I could take a breath and say, "I made it. I'm a good person who is loved now." But it never came, because life kept moving on in the same patterns. *Why was I waiting for an endpoint to feel valued? Wasn't life about living?*

At the time, it was more important for me to follow guidelines and society's path than to follow my own. I strove to make everyone happy by keeping my head down and doing what I was told. What started brewing was a perfect storm of unhappiness. Joy was a distant thought, and I was hardly in a situation in which I was listening to my own inner wisdom. I was out of touch with myself and what I liked. I was a stranger to myself, and it felt like I was falling deeper and deeper into the dark shell of a human I once was.

I vividly remember my first day at my corporate job. Sitting at my desk, I looked around and said, "Is this it?" Four years in high school, five years of university, and two years of volunteering and working multiple jobs to finally get into a career position (because everyone wanted to hire people with experience). This was it. This was the day society said I'd been working toward my whole life. It was also the beginning of my decline.

I looked around at my options for growth in the company and saw people who were miserable, constantly speaking negatively, living for weekends and their one vacation a year, arguing about benefits and what the company and the government owed them. "Is this really it?" I kept thinking to myself. "Is this the life that everyone says is why I'm on this earth?"

I fell into the routine that surrounded me. I waited for Fridays, dreaded Mondays, and lived for the next stage in life to check off my list, hoping that that next stage would be the thing that finally brought me happiness. My life existed to follow what everyone else thought I should do, which made me look ambitious and hardworking. All the while, my health and well-being were non-existent, and I didn't have any self-worth or confidence. I felt lost in a sea of anxiety and sadness, but I didn't know why. No one had prepared me for anguish. They had only prepared me to fit me into a box, which I gladly crawled into.

All of this gave room for anxiety, stress, and depression to grow and expand. Mental illness was feeding and growing off its own existence. The further I wandered from my true self and the things that naturally brought me joy, the worse I became.

*And who was my true self?* She was a powerful and explorative twelve-year-old girl. She was wild, she was expansive, free, and feminine — in all the best ways. I realized something key: for my survival, for my own sanity, and healing, *I* needed to make changes to learn how to be my own best friend. No one would make the changes for me or know what I needed, and I chose to no longer be a victim of circumstance. I got real with myself and started looking into what I liked doing when no one was watching. *What did I want in life? What kind of lifestyle brought me joy? What made me smile, with no purpose at all?*

I got wild.

I quit my career job and in secret asked for a job at the local bistro in a small town. I needed to run and break free, somewhere where no one knew me or had expectations from me. I wanted to start again. I began trying new things and exploring different career paths. I know how it looks to people when I explain that I've been a flight attendant, a veterinary hospital receptionist, a volunteer and donations manager, a retail manager, a wedding planner, a marketing manager, and a blog editor and entrepreneur with a degree in criminology with a minor in policing and domestic violence.

I know that some people, family, and friends may not *get* me and may question why I don't stick to one thing. I've just been wildly explorative in the most "color-outside-the-lines" kind of way. I tried their way, *and I wasn't happy.* I'm the one living this life, and I'm the one who gets to make choices without worrying about what people have to say. I've tried living a life that waited for fleeting moments of joy, and I didn't have the strength to survive in it. I'm eternally grateful for my *perceived* weakness in joyless situations, because it's not a weakness at all: it's my superpower. It sparked a self-discovery journey that I am still on, and I will never be done. I consider it my job here on this earth to live, to discover . . . to be *wild*.

My quest for living in joy every day has developed through my wild feminine nature. My femininity is my power, and my wildness is my strength. The days when I don't wake up in joy are the days when I start the work to find out what my body, mind, and soul need. There have been countless tools, negative cycles, and things uncovered.

Through all of this, although I was a product of circumstances, I take full responsibility for the part I played in finding comfort in following the crowd. I could have stood up for myself. I could have said no. And I could have changed my trajectory much sooner.

That's the beauty of free will.

I blame no one, not even myself. Now I only see a story to tell to help show others who feel the way I did: that there is another way.

## Go Back to Go Forward

Isn't it interesting that as children, we are vibrant beacons of joy who delight in the simplest pleasures yet as we grow older, we have to work at being happy? Somewhere along the way, I lost touch with myself. One of the tools that I am working with now is reconnecting with my inner child. That child that you look back on is still you. You didn't magically become a different human being altogether. You are still a child. Age does not change what most ignites you inside. There is no age at which we cease being children to *someone*, so why do we disassociate ourselves from the label?

At the start, it was too difficult to ask myself what brought me joy and made me happy in the present moment. It was much easier to think back to when I was a child and explore what *delighted* me then. What did it look like, smell like, and feel like? The day that I silenced my imagination and decided to grow up is the day I lost a piece of me. It's the day that I stopped listening to my intuition.

When you're a child, that's all you have — your instinct, your wisdom, and your gut feeling. "I like this, and I don't like that." You are still untainted by society's description of what you should and shouldn't do or like. We are born wild.

We often look back on old childhood photos of ourselves and cringe in embarrassment. But that's *still you*. Would you feel the same if you looked at a picture of an innocent child that wasn't you? I made a point to go through old photo albums and pick a photo that represented the essence of who I was. Not the cutest photo, but the one in which I was more raw and vulnerable. I now carry it around with me and have it in my office. I look at it once a week and strive to listen to that little girl and ask her, "What would you like to do?"

By reconnecting to my inner child, I realized how much I missed being playful, adventurous, and imaginative. I used to have courage, be spontaneous, and create worlds with my mind. All I had was a snack in my overalls and a walking stick in my hand, and I was joyous. I used to love going on hiking adventures in the woods or swimming all day until my mom swore I became a fish. As I grew up, I became too concerned about becoming sweaty or having to re-do my hair to look presentable in public. I stopped playing because sitting poised in a chair was safer.

This year, it was time to make the changes, and I've been listening to that little girl. I joined a baseball league and a golf league. I've been swimming more in the last week than I have in the last five years. I've spontaneously been going on adventures in nature, and I've been gentle with myself when I need it. I've reconnected with my inner child to get back to living wildly in my mind, to let it wander and delight in unruly nature.

When I was a child, I didn't think of failure before I played a game. I just jumped in and did it. I believed in myself without consequence. Recently, I've been working on going outside my comfort zone without thinking about the outcome — like writing this chapter. It's being vulnerable, raw, real, wild, and free. I started writing this chapter for no one else but myself because it felt good.

## It's Already in You

I often looked for acceptance and love all around me, whether this was from my priest, my parents, my teacher, my boss, my friends, or my family. If I was a good person and followed the rules, I would have their acceptance and love. The cycle was self-destructive and was also setting them up for disappointing me when they didn't live up to my standards of how I wanted them to accept me. It wasn't their fault. I was always chasing something, working toward something, and trying to get to the next step of something. Nothing and no one was feeding the hunger that I had to live a happy life. When I began to take steps toward curating a life of joy, I explored the idea that I am already everything I need. I don't need anyone else's approval, acceptance,or a pat on the back in order to feel unconditional love for myself. I was chasing joy through these people, and I didn't even know it (nor did they). I know now that I *am* joy.

Anxiety flared up when I looked forward, and depression greeted me when I remembered the past. My brain automatically gravitated toward memories of failure, missed opportunities, or fear of the unknown. Even the happy times caused me pain and torment. I used to look back at a memory in fondness and appreciation more often than feeling those feelings in the moment the memory was happening. I would also look back at the same memory in sadness because it was over and I missed it. I simultaneously reminisced in joy and sadness, creating a growth of depression in my thought patterns.

By noticing these thoughts as they show up, letting them go with love, and replacing them with one of current joy, I would break the pattern. I am able to teach my brain to focus on things that make me smile in the present moment. I try to apply this method to other negative or anxious reoccurrences when my old tendencies resurface. If anything, I've learned that nothing happens overnight and growth comes from trial and error. I try different things all the time and have fun exploring the wild possibilities that await me. I already have everything I need within me. It's now about delighting in the discovery of everything and healing the bruises so that I can get up and continue my journey to embracing my full feminine power.

When I was young, time seemed to move so slowly. It has only gained momentum and passed by increasingly faster as I've aged. A family member once told me that this happens because when we're babies, we live moment by moment. As we grow a little more and move into elementary school, we live day by day. In high school, we live weekend by weekend. In university, we live month by month. And in our career, we plan vacation time and live year by year through a series of milestones. I know now that my life is about the journey and what's happening right now. It's not about what will happen tomorrow or what happened yesterday. Truly, life's potential should be measured in its second-by-second sequence, not the sum of all parts.

Understanding the power of mindfulness and being in the present moment has changed my life. Mindfulness has become a close friend of mine, especially helpful when anxiety or depression flare up or as a way to truly experience life. I want to show people that it's possible to be in joy through listening to your intuition, reconnecting with your younger self, paying attention to the moment, and curating, with intention, the life that you want to live. Waiting for someone else's validation or confirmation will not bring joy. I trust myself, my wisdom, *and my weaknesses*. I am worthy of the life I want, without needing to fit society's norms of success, hiding my femininity, or taming my inner wild child.

Now I color outside the lines.

The moment I let go of the pencil I was holding onto so tightly for perfection and embraced my natural instincts of wild femininity is the moment I met myself again. I am the only thing that held me back from my internal power and strength — and now I have fun exploring externally what it means to be a woman.

I have no regrets, and I surround myself with joy at every turn. My life will never be perfect, nor do I wish it to be, because that just sounds like another rose-colored box.

# VULNERABILITY

# IS NOT A SIGN

# OF WEAKNESS.

UNLEASHING HER WILD

# CHAPTER 03

# FINDING SOUL:

# THE JOURNEY THROUGH TRAUMA TO DISCOVERING TRUE SELF

## BY: RENEE KAYLOR

*"No more silence, no more hiding behind twisted pain. Discover the power and feel our collective courage gaining strength within every woman."*

# RENEE KAYLOR

〜〜〜〜〜〜

ig: @reneekaylor

www.reneekaylor.ca

As an artist, creative, free spirit, and wildly optimistic soul, Renee Kaylor believes life is a journey of spiritual and personal development. Renee graduated with distinction from the University of Calgary with a bachelor's degree in psychology and a minor in fine arts, while also achieving First Team All-Canadian in athletics. Combining her background in athletics, arts, and psychology, Renee has developed the unique ability to coach women through a journey of self-discovery and to embrace their inner power and wild beauty.

Renee's insatiable thirst for exploration, combined with her disciplined drive for high achievement, has proven to be rewarding. Her passion for life has no boundaries. She was the first woman in her high school's history to win a State Championship in athletics and was also named "Best in the City" by Toronto Life for her fashion styling.

Renee currently resides in Toronto, the city she has lovingly called home for more than a decade. When she is not working with her clients, you can find Renee enjoying one of her many other creative passions: sketching in the park, working on her next writing project, developing a new character at an acting studio, or flying through the air on aerial silks. Look out for what's next from this always energetic, wild woman.

**L**ight dimmed in my eyes, my body lifeless, my mind littered with self-hatred: it took pain to guide me toward a much-needed change and to seek out the lessons that I needed to learn. Emotionally, I was stripped down to nothing. It was drastic yet entirely necessary for me to create space to heal. I was in a job I hated with an abusive partner. I had moved three times that year, trying to find somewhere to call home. I was disconnected from my body, mind, and spirit. It had been this way for a year before I finally felt the Universe open up and swallow me whole. The day my partner was arrested and charged with domestic assault was the day everything in my life fell apart. It took two strangers witnessing him assaulting me in public, as well as a caring detective, for me to finally stop this cycle of abuse. While it was incredibly painful, I am grateful for it today. Over the last year, I have found a way to put the pieces back together. While I am a work in progress, I am certain that I am finally on the path of creating my life with purpose.

I felt the weight of the world. It was heavy; everything I believed, everything I subscribed to, the people around me, all felt foreign. None of it fit. I felt like I was playing a part in someone else's life. It wasn't my own. *How did I even end up here?* I looked closely and realized the six-figure income in a job where I felt completely disconnected was suffocating my spirit. The partner I had chosen had broken me down to the point I didn't recognize who I had become. Have you ever had that feeling of being completely lost and not sure how you ended up in the life you find yourself living?

I stared into the mirror and didn't recognize the person staring back. The light was gone from my eyes. They were lifeless and devoid of any emotion. It was the strangest feeling. I thought I knew who I was. I was a planner; I participated in every decision; each moment when I had a choice, I was the one choosing. Yet here I was, looking into the vacant eyes of a complete stranger. I felt an overwhelmingly deep despair for this shell of a woman standing across from me. I could no longer see my own soul. I had submerged her in all of this chaos.

Years prior, I found meditation. I had begun to take care of my spirit for the first time, and it had a profoundly positive impact on my life. At one time, I had been connected. Yet here I stood, nearly ten years later, unable to recognize myself, unable to see my soul. Everything felt out of place. I examined what I spent my time on, who I spent my time with, where I spent my money. I realized it was spent on all the wrong things, with the wrong people. I was not in line with my life path, and I knew so strongly that it was time to finally make adjustments in all aspects of my life. I had been neglecting my spirit, ignoring the Universe's direction, and she was screaming to be heard. Instinctually, I was drawn to take a journey alone to find that vibrant woman I once knew. I felt the process of being alone was necessary to reconnect with nature and open my spiritual journey to discover my authentic self.

> *"Most of the time this major theft creeps up on the person from their blind side. It comes upon women . . . because of naivete, poor insight into the motives of others, inexperienced in projecting what might happen in the future, not paying attention to all the clues in the environment, and because fate is always weaving lessons into the weft."*
> ~ Clarissa Pinkola Estes

Looking back, it is clear now how naïve and overly optimistic I had been. Each time my partner said he wouldn't hurt me again, each time he blamed me for making him angry, for pushing him too far. Each time his body towered over mine, his eyes raging with fire, his hands digging into my flesh, while I begged him to stop. I forgave him with a blind love while he systematically chipped away at my power, dimming my once flourishing bright light. It crept up on me slowly. One day I was left with a deep self-loathing, an overwhelming feeling of worthlessness, drained of my once vibrant life. I put on a mask for the outside world, believing I could hide the truth, while I continued to fall deeper into the darkness.

This was all too familiar. Dark moments from my childhood returned. The images and words attached to the pain that I pushed deep down now found a way back to my consciousness. The screaming, the beatings, the blood, the police, the hospitals, the safe houses: all of it flooded my mind and paralyzed my body. I revisited these past traumas as the cycle continued. I kept ignoring the signs the Universe desperately tried to show me, each time believing I deserved to be treated this way. Believing that I was as worthless as he said because I had been told I was nothing so many times before. It was always there, lurking beneath the surface. I was vulnerable, an easy target for others to feed on. I was a body wandering through life without soul, guided only by a willful spirit and an overcompensating ego.

Others can see our light; they are drawn to our life force, spirit, or soul. When that light is taken from us, we have to embark on a journey of rediscovery. In order to break free from the darkness, we must find our way back to the source of our light. For me, this meant traveling back home to the California coast, renting a campervan, and hitting the road for a solo trip with just me and my dog, Pippa. I didn't have a return flight. I didn't even have a destination. My only set plan was to pick up a van in Vegas and drive into the desert. I made this decision one exceptionally painful day, at the end of a difficult month. My body was drained and frail, my mind abnormally unfocused, and my spirit completely broken. My light, my inner Being, my identity was gone. I was an empty shell of the woman I once embodied.

Following my intuition, the call from within me to reconnect, I felt a desire to seek out my truth. I went into the woods to heal my wounds alone, independently. Not knowing the next step, I followed a strong instinctual drive, one day at a time. I flowed, blowing with the winds on the California coast, searching for something I left behind many years before.

At the beginning of the trip, I was drawn to the Grand Canyon. I had never been there before nor had I ever felt a desire to go. Yet for some reason, it called to me now. I arrived in darkness to a campground near the South Rim. The temperature was dropping while I built a fire for the first time. I was grateful for the warmth and satisfaction of managing on my own. As the fire dimmed, Pippa became frightened and tense as a pack of wolves or coyotes happily howled. I fell asleep to the howling, and, when I awoke a few hours later from the cold, it was silent. I opened the curtains to a white blanket of snow covering the world around me. I'll never forget how beautiful the forest looked covered in snow, or how bright it was with the moon shining on the falling snowflakes. I felt instantly relaxed and connected. I felt I knew I was on the right path.

I spent one more day there, driving the South Rim, stopping to take in the incredible views, and enjoying a little hike down the canyon. Then it was back to the desert. I made an overnight stop at a campground in the Mojave Desert. As I turned off the main highway and drove into the open sand-covered land, I felt lonely. The endless desert, and not seeing any other vehicles or people as the sun got closer to the horizon, made me feel overwhelmingly alone. When I arrived at the campground, it was nearly empty; only two other sites were occupied. That night as I went to bed, I left a curtain open, facing east across the desert. In the morning, I woke to one of the most beautiful sunrises I've ever experienced. It made me feel alive and hopeful: a reminder that every day is a gift.

I felt a necessary pull to visit my grandpa and found my next stop at his lovely home near Palm Springs. I had not stayed at his home in years. Now I felt I needed to visit him and to stay in the room where I always felt welcomed and loved. I slept so peacefully that night and woke to my grandpa making pancakes in the shape of animals — a tradition from my early childhood. I was beyond touched that he would still do this for me. It brought back so many wonderful memories of the unconditional love he provided. He was my rock, the person I looked up to most in my life, never wanting to let him down. That visit meant everything to me because it was the last happy visit we had before he passed away a couple of months later. My grandpa reminded me that I was loved, that I had great value to others in my life, and that I had a place to call home. He always had a way of making me believe everything would be okay and that I could and would make it to the other side of things stronger than before.

After I left my grandpa's house, I headed toward the coast to visit family and friends and connect with those I loved. I was able to briefly enjoy the comforts of home by the beach before heading north toward my unknown destination. It was New Year's Eve and I found myself on a beach in Malibu. The last moments of the year were marked with chaos, pain, and pieces being stripped away. What a perfect way to end this chapter: to end the year of abuse and suffering with another man dominating me, his body towering over my small frame. The Universe needed to remind me, to make it really clear, why I was on this journey. I fell for it this one last time. Pulled into the frenzy of his desire, his intense sexual power over me was familiar, intoxicating. He grabbed me, he kissed me, and I did not resist. He was too hungry, too fast. I felt pain course through my body. Familiar pain that I had attached to pleasure: domination of my body from careless masculine energy overpowering my fragile being.

For a moment, I am not in my body. I see it clearly, this theft and a piece of my soul being taken. There was another predator tearing at my flesh, ripping apart my spirit, and leaving scars on my psyche. The damage done, I quietly retreated to the comfort of my traveling home. In the morning, I woke to the sun dancing on my face through the curtains. Peeking out, I saw the waves rumbling toward me, washing over the sand, leaving behind a brilliant, shimmering glow of diamonds on the beach. That morning, at the beginning of a new year, Mother Nature was my guide as I ran into the ocean and dove under the icy cold waves. The water cleansed my body of the trauma. Emerging from the healing water, I felt hope as power returned to my spirit.

Next the journey called me to the magical land of the sequoias. Walking through a forest of these giants, I felt so small and yet deeply connected to everything around me. I continued to head north, winding my way through the Sierra Nevada mountains to Yosemite. I had never been, yet much like the Grand Canyon, now I was strongly drawn to visit. My arrival at Yosemite was breathtaking. The impact of this part of the journey was intense: surrounded by the giant mountains, through the giant trees, the big world surrounding me, I was shown a greater picture of the world long before me. I strongly felt a part of my soul deeply connected to this place. I left Yosemite feeling lighter, a piece of my soul restored.

I was drawn back to the coast, through Carmel, to Big Sur. Once I arrived, I knew this was my destination. Big Sur was a place I often found myself during cycles of change in my life. This quiet town is nestled in the shade of redwoods high above the violent waters of the Pacific, on the rocky edge of my homeland. Each time I felt empty, disconnected, and lonely, I found myself there. Over the endless sea of dark blue, as the sun reached the horizon, it lit the sky on fire and cast a rosy glow on the Santa Lucia mountains. The sun reached deep into my core, restoring the warmth, the light I had lost.

That night I floated naked in the healing waters of the natural hot springs under a blanket of stars, listening to the waves crashing on the cliffs below. Alone, peaceful, connected: I was finally free of that deep-rooted pain. That was the night I rediscovered her, that Wild Feminine woman. This moment in my life was one of the most profound transformations. Every part of this journey was leading here. I followed my instincts, I allowed the Universe to guide me, and I found my soul. I was finally able to quiet my mind, heal my body, and find my light. Yes, it was painful at first. It was lonely. I was forced to examine my life from the inside out, to dig up past traumas, and to face the pain of the past year. In the end, it was all necessary to discover the incredible woman I am.

At some point in life, we all feel our light dimmed, our direction lost, our strength and power weakened. I encourage you to take the journey, take the time alone, to heal with guidance from the Universe. Listen to the call from within. Be open to facing challenges that come up along the way and learn the lessons required to move forward. If we allow our defenses to hold us back from discovering our power, we will continue in a loop of our past. The most difficult experiences create the possibility to learn profoundly important lessons in life, if we are prepared to take the journey. Are you ready to break free from past traumas and worry of an uncertain future? Take a deep breath and be alive in the moment, right now. I encourage you to seek out your light source, your wild woman, and discover your authentic self. It is in your control. Reality is what we make it.

Today I am living this transformation. Each day I am more in love with my life and appreciative of my journey into the woods. The Universe guided me, opened my mind, cleansed my body, and freed me psychologically and spiritually. I gained the ability to love myself in a way I didn't know possible and to connect to the world around me on a deeply powerful level.

Together, we can take the leap of faith, trust in the Universe, trust in our journey, and embrace the waves of pain coursing through our bodies as we strip down to the core of our being. This pain is our path to growth. Only when we truly journey to the root, buried deep within our soul, are we given the ability to see, to feel, and to heal. Only then can the Wild Feminine emerge and guide us on the journey of rebuilding, carefully, one moment at a time, until our light is once again shining bright.

# UNLEASH

# YOUR

# CREATIVITY

---

UNLEASHING HER WILD

# CHAPTER 04

# WILDLY PASSIONATE, DEEPLY SURRENDERED, FIERCELY FREE

BY: DANIELLE LAURA

*"There is no power quite like that of a woman, in full surrender, and trust of, her divine intuition."*

# DANIELLE LAURA

ig: @_daniellelaura_ | fb: @Daniellelauracoaching
www.danielle-laura.com

Danielle is a mission-driven former corporate medical executive turned spiritual entrepreneur. She has spent the last decade innovating therapy work, in addition to leading teams of change makers, which gives her an exceptional understanding of human behavior and what it takes for lasting transformation and success at every level. As the CEO and Founder of H.O.T. Souls™ Individual and Couples Coaching, Danielle is passionate about helping people shift their entire paradigm, live fully expressed lives, and make their greatest impact. Her mission is to help change makers ground into their truth, master their gifting in order to amplify their zone of genius, cultivate H.O.T., thriving relationships, and up-level their life in transformative ways. Danielle has a master's degree in counseling and a bachelor's degree in health science and is a certified Reiki Master.

There comes a point in our lives when we realize we're on the brink of transformation: the kind that will change the trajectory of our world. We feel the fire burning in our hearts for more. We may not even fully know what "more" is in that moment, but we know whatever it is, we need it. It's the itching to follow every call that excites our spirit, to do the things that defy all logic because we believe something magical is waiting for us. It's the day we choose to be the leading lady in our own life and unwaveringly trust our divine feminine intuition that our life seemingly changes forever.

*"If you plan on being anything less than you are truly capable of being, you will probably be unhappy all the days of your life."*[1]

I answered the soul call, the call of my spirit, to intentionally choose to let my God-given intuition lead me, every single day. After years of underrating my inner knowing and letting the thoughts, feelings, energy, and opinions of others dictate my decisions, I finally decided to break free. I was so busy trying to make the world a more beautiful place that my own soul was a battleground. *What did I need? What did I want? How was I truly meant to serve in this world?*

I tuned in, looked my fears in the eye, and surrendered every tear-soaked prayer to God to lead me on the journey of my soul-driven mission in this world. I knew that every answer I would ever need was already within me. I also knew that it was my choice whether to listen and follow accordingly. What did my soul whisper? It told me I needed to get grounded into the truth of my being, and never look back. And so I did. I left my stable corporate career as a medical executive, took the leap of faith

---

1    Maslow, Abraham. (n.d.). Goodreads. Retrieved from https://www.goodreads.com/quotes/341532-if-you-plan-on-being-anything-less-than-you-are

into entrepreneurship, kissed the manipulation of others good-bye, and set sail on my highest path.

If you're anything like me, your divine intuition has probably thrown you for a loop your entire life. You have probably underrated your inner knowing and let people-pleasing and perfectionism be your compass, leading you into an endless cycle of depletion, burnout, and persistent longing for more. After so many years of silencing your own soul for the sake of others, you meet yourself at a crossroads where you can continue down the lane of "shoulds" and "what if's" or you can choose to shift your entire paradigm and blaze your own trail in total surrender and trust.

You have the power to choose to live the highest and best path of your life, allowing you to make your greatest impact on the rise of humanity.

On a Wednesday night, I sat on my bedroom floor, looking out the window up to the sky with outstretched arms and an open heart, and prayed, "I surrender, God. I surrender my path for the highest path meant for me. Use me to change this world, and remove from my life anything or anyone hindering my ability to do so. Give me eyes to see, ears to hear, and the courage to accept every call that is meant for me. I trust. I surrender."

I'm not sure what I thought would happen next; perhaps a rainbow would appear in the sky . . . Little did I know in that moment, I was embarking on the spiritual journey that would forever change my life. When we decide to surrender to our highest good, to unwaveringly trust the inner wisdom of our divine intuition, our faith is put to the test. When we surrender the comfort zone of our old paradigm and take each next divinely guided step, we may be led to do some really scary things that defy all logic and common sense. Life may get messy. Trials can come our way that either make us question everything and stay "safe" in our comfort zone or solidify our faith deeper than ever as we jump and trust that the net will appear. In the months following that night, I learned that the more I was tested, the more I knew I could trust.

As I began my journey of connecting and opening my heart to receive goodness, ease, flow, and joy into my life, change became my constant and my world flipped upside down overnight. While I was building my business and mastering my spiritual gifting, slander and attacks ensued. I was accused of doing absurd things, friends turned their backs on me, I had every penny stolen out of my bank account, my marriage ended in a divorce, and I had to move houses and find a new church and community.

Any of these things alone would have been enough to make someone fall apart, to give up, and to just turn back to live the life that's "safe." I remember talking to my mentor and saying, "What the actual hell?! I surrendered! Why is my life falling apart?!" And *that* is when my spirit answered, "It's falling into place. Trust the process. Be at peace." While a lot of days were emotionally draining and consisted of some of the most difficult times of my entire life as I lost everything I had clung to so dearly, an internal miracle was taking place. I was able to be at total peace in the midst of the chaotic storm around me. I made it through each trying day with grace because I knew my steps were divinely guided. I realized that everything was happening *for* me, not *to* me, and all was well with my soul. I firmly believe that the grace in which I handled this quantum shift of my life can be attributed to several practices of embodiment that allowed me to stay grounded and secure in my being, deepening an unshakable faith and further allowing me to fiercely trust my inner compass.

Grounding into your truth is the foundation to unwaveringly and unapologetically trusting your intuition and divine mission. To help you get clear about what this might look like, write out your core truths and beliefs, the values by which you live your life. Take time to feel into them with all of your heart. Ask yourself, "What is true for me? Who does God say I am? Who do I believe I am? How do I show up in this world as a result of that?"

When you're able to have clarity on who you are, it becomes much easier to make decisions that are in alignment for you. This is the time when you choose to rise and thrive. This means getting super raw with yourself and uncovering the "why" behind your why. It means summoning the courage to release anything inhibiting you from standing achieving it. It's about getting crystal clear on your soul-driven mission, which requires being H.O.T. (honest, open, and transparent) with yourself. It's about facing fears and doubts head on and choosing not to distract, suppress, or replace any emotion you feel. Instead, you can create a new pattern to heal these old beliefs. A beautiful exercise to support you in this is to reframe your limiting belief by creating a different, true story; this rewires a new pattern in your mind.

For example, a fear that came up for me was: *If I stand in my truth and make decisions by trusting my intuition, some people may not get it and choose to leave my life.* I re-framed this to: *When I stand in my truth and trust my intuition, I will build soul connections with those who resonate with my authenticity, and I will always be guided and supported.* When you are grounded in the truth of your own value and how you uniquely serve in this world, you won't be swayed by the opinions of others. Instead you will understand your own worthiness and will be at peace in your own soul. From there, you must respect yourself enough to establish strong boundaries so that you can continue to pour from a full cup. Ask yourself what you need as a non-negotiable every day in order to thrive emotionally, mentally, spiritually, and physically, and incorporate this into your self-care routine.

The next golden pieces on my journey to trusting my divine intuition were meditation, prayer, and journaling. Meditation is key to allowing yourself to be centered and in tune with your body, thoughts, and emotions. We must get quiet in order to hear, and in order to heal, we must feel. Meditation helps us recognize what is our own and what we've taken on from someone else. It brings a keen awareness to the stillness and helps us to clearly understand how our intuition speaks to us. Being aware of how we receive intuitive downloads is important to notice, too; we may see an image or symbol, hear actual guidance, have a word pop into our brain, or even just feel something deeply in our body. Take note of how the information comes through for you, as *this* may be the dominant way your intuition speaks to you. Knowing this will provide you with greater clarity.

During, or even after, meditation and prayer, journaling can be a beautiful outlet for divine downloads to come through you. An exercise you can try today is called free writing. To do this, write without thinking until you feel led to stop. As you write, allow your heart to open freely and let the words flow out of you. Go back and re-read the messages of your heart. You'll likely be amazed at the Divine goodness of truth pouring out of you, often giving you the exact answers you need.

There is also truth to the expression, *"Your energy doesn't lie."* Being fiercely protective of your energy is a crucial aspect of trusting your intuition. If you're reading this book, you're probably an empath, one who feels the emotion, energy, and vibration of others and situations. As empaths, we are prone to taking on the energy of others as our own, which can sometimes result in extreme emotional highs and lows. These feelings can come seemingly out of nowhere because we care so much and feel everything so deeply. If we aren't careful or aware of what is our own energy and what isn't, we can succumb to a cycle of depletion. It's vital to cleanse, ground, and protect our energy daily. I believe this practice is what helped me to remain grounded and as peaceful as possible during my tumultuous trials.

To cleanse your energy, get into a meditative state and visualize a bright white light or a clear waterfall moving from the top of your head down through each of the meridian centers in your body, down through your legs, and out of your feet into the Earth. To ground your energy, visualize roots coming out of the bottom of your feet and going deep into the Earth. You can also visualize an anchor coming out of your feet or the base of your spine and cementing your foundation into Mother Earth. To protect your energy for the day, visualize a bright golden bubble of light surrounding your energy field. You can also visualize yourself in a diamond hedge of protection, free from harm. When you have cleansed, grounded, and protected your energy, you'll notice that you're able to clearly be in tune with your intuition. It should be free of any barriers that could be clouding it, and you will discover that you will not take on others' emotions as your own.

Next, chase your joy. Any time you are experiencing joy, you are connecting to the flow state in which your intuition thrives. This is a beautiful embodiment practice: find your creative flow, what lights you up, and do just that. Maybe it's spending time in nature, dancing, writing, or taking beautiful photographs. Connect to your creative center, and you'll unlock an undeniably powerful intuitive force.

Three questions that might be helpful in connecting you to joy are: *What would make me feel alive today? What inspired action can I take to achieve this? How can I make this a pleasurable experience?* These questions can help you connect your head (thoughts and actions) to your heart (emotions and desires) in order to create intentional, optimal, intuitive success.

There is no power quite like that of a woman in full surrender and trust of her divine intuition. Every time we choose to trust with wild abandon, we heal ourselves and are then able to use our medicine to help heal the world. Choosing to set flames to the status quo by leaning into our feminine essence and surrendering expectation takes immense courage, bold faith, and an unparalleled inner resiliency. Yes, we will experience trials that feel like they are going to break us. Yes, we will have to make decisions that scare the daylights out of us. Yes, we will have to defeat heartbreak and experience hurt that strikes us to our core . . . But above all, when we tune in, we welcome the most potently powerful, deeply fulfilling possibilities that will surpass our wildest imagination.

Being on the other side of the paradigm shift of my life, I can tell you with absolute conviction that every single minute of the heartache and strife of losing my old self to welcome my highest self was worth it. When you trust the divinity within you, you welcome more freedom, passion, time, connection, authenticity, impact, and abundance into your world.

I was able to foster my spiritual and intuitive gifts, deepen my zone of genius, and develop higher levels of consciousness. I was able to turn my self-sacrificing patterns into self-mastery and release people-pleasing once and for all. I shattered my own limiting beliefs and healed wounds I didn't even realize I had. I gained a skyrocketed confidence in my truth and mission that allowed me to welcome my heart's desires into life. In turn, I have a deeper self-love and a stronger inner empowerment than ever before. I finally feel in harmony within my mind, body, and spirit.

Your best guide is inside. Whatever trial you may be facing, know that you can turn your perceived weakness into your greatest superpower. You can live the most fully expressed life that sets your soul on fire. Decide that the most wildly passionate, deeply surrendered, and fiercely free life is right in front of you, because it is. Surrender, trust, tune in, take inspired action, repeat.

# SHARE

# YOUR

# SELF

UNLEASHING HER WILD

# CHAPTER 05

# FINDING YOUR FREEDOM THROUGH PLEASURE AND ORGASM

BY: ELENI GRAY

*"Healing shame and stored emotion in the body is the missing piece that women need to heal, allow themselves to receive love in their life, and be seen for who they really are."*

# ELENI GRAY

~~~~~~

fb: @xoelenigray

www.eleni-gray.com

Eleni Gray is a women's empowerment coach, healer, and dedicated mother and wife. Eleni helps people heal past trauma, find balance in their lives, and expand into the highest version of themselves in their life and business. She believes that anyone has the ability to create the life of their dreams by dedicating themselves to their own healing, self-love, and self-care.

Eleni is an entrepreneur, has a successful online business, and is sought after by women all over the world for her gifts, talents, and healing abilities. She is able to hold sacred space for people, prides herself in being a voice for change in the world, and creates impact in the areas she feels deeply passionate about.

W hen women feel free in their bodies, they create the space to be able to hold the frequency of the Divine Feminine. They stand in their power, they allow themselves to be seen for who they truly are, and they are able to give birth to new creations from a place of deep self-love. This is rejuvenating and restorative for a woman's entire mental, emotional, physical, spiritual, and energetic being.

In Western culture, however, women experience much confusion around our sexuality and our bodies. Sex is everywhere, yet there is still such a strong belief that our sexuality, our ability to feel pleasure in our bodies through orgasm, is wrong or dirty and that it must only be used for a few moments of stress relief or instant gratification. Even the word "vagina" is uncomfortable for many women to hear. Topics such as sexual abuse have been swept under the rug, and we have been taught and told for generations not to speak up about our feelings, abuse, and pain.

We have been told to keep quiet and do as we are told so that we do not cause a stir or bring attention to ourselves in case, God forbid, we shame our families, society, and everybody around us. How can we, as women, allow ourselves to be fully expressed in all of who we are if we are taught to feel ashamed of who we are?

It is just as important to care for and nourish a woman's sacred sexuality and body as the other areas of her life. By healing and connecting to her body, a woman will discover that the freedom she has been deeply searching for was always within her. Doing so allows her to receive all of the pleasures that life has to offer: pleasures that she rightfully deserves. The rise of the Divine Feminine shows us that we need to all rise together to shed light on our wounds. When we consciously connect to the core of our being, we heal the parts of ourselves where we hold shame and give ourselves permission to feel liberated and ecstatic. This also includes sending love to our vaginas from our hearts. It is in *this* space that we, as women, will find our way back to ourselves and our authentic truth.

So what is it that stops us from receiving love and pleasure in our lives? What prevents us from being open and trusting our intuition? What hinders our ability to deepen our intimacy with our partners? More importantly, what holds us back from deepening the intimacy and pleasure that we have with ourselves? What stops us from setting strong boundaries with others? Why do we resist allowing ourselves to truly shine our light without the guilt, shame, and self-sabotage in between? The answer: shame, unprocessed stored emotion, and lack of self-love.

Feeling and emotion is an aspect of the Divine Feminine that allows us to receive and stay in balance with our masculine. The masculine side of ourselves is very productive in getting things done and is our action-taker. Our feminine side is receptive and always in flow. She is our nurturer, our connection to our sexuality, our bodies, and our truth; she holds an energy that is both fiercely soft and fiercely loving. She is our inner child who brings playfulness into our lives. She is our queen who sets firm but loving boundaries, our wise woman who holds ancient knowledge and guides us on our path in life. She is not weak, like many perceive her to be, nor is she is overbearing. The Divine Feminine is ultimately a powerful force that, when in balance with the masculine, has the ability to move mountains.

## What Storing Shame and Unprocessed Emotion Can Do to a Person's Life

As a young woman, I was highly intuitive and very sensitive to the energies around me. I was also very disconnected from feeling pleasure within myself and within my own body. I was always looking to please and nurture everyone else rather then nurturing myself or allowing myself to feel love or joy.

My downhill spiral began in my early twenties. I found myself in a bar one night and my drink was spiked. I was raped. My body was unable to move or speak, while my higher self lay there still, in shock, screaming with all her might, "Get off of me!" I remember that night vividly. I remember stumbling home looking disheveled and a mess. I remember a car full of people pulling over on the side of the road asking me if I needed help. I also remember insisting I was okay and making my way home alone.

I mentally blocked out parts of this night and didn't fully deal with the pain until nine years later when my shame, resentment, passive aggressive nature, and mistrust in men almost led my husband and I to get divorced.

My body literally couldn't hold the shadow and shame in my body anymore. Memories of abuse were continually surfacing, and I felt like I was losing my mind. What was actually happening was a call for healing, a call for resolution from my higher self. You see, my higher self was ready to deal with the traumatic events that had occurred in my life, and the emotions that were surfacing as anger, rage, sadness, and depression were my body's way of saying, "Eleni, it is time." My body was ready to be loved. My soul was screaming for healing and my intuition was leading the way the whole time.

When a woman's body stores shame and pain from the past, she will feel like she isn't being seen in her life. She will feel deeply disconnected from her pleasure, feel guilty in times when she feels good about herself or beautiful, and not allow herself to shine out of a fear that others around her may not feel good or beautiful as well.

She will self-sabotage relationships with men and others due to her fear of intimacy and unworthiness to receive love She will not allow herself to receive money in her business and/or to truly feel the joy of receiving deep love. In truth, if a woman isn't allowing herself to receive love in one area of her life, she isn't allowing herself to receive love in other areas of her life either. So many women are such amazing givers but are resistant when it comes to receiving. For example, say you are an entrepreneur and currently run a business that you love; the amount of money that you charge for your services and manifest into your business is a direct reflection of how much love you allow yourself to receive. Money is merely a form of energy that is reflective of how much you value who you are and what you have to offer. If you felt unloved as a child or experienced traumatic events which you haven't fully healed from, the emotional pain will still be stored in your body. You will have a block in allowing yourself to feel and receive pleasure until you clear the trauma on a mind, body, and soul level. This pattern will continue to show up in your life, perhaps as self-sabotaging your success or reaching a certain point in your business that you cannot seem to move past. *This* is why so many people walk around living life in their heads, totally disconnected from their bodies: for them, feeling is too painful.

Much of the pain we experience in life is due to trapped emotions and unprocessed life experiences that we hold within our nervous system. The symptoms of depression, stress, anxiety, and lack of self-love is the body crying out and talking to us, telling us that there is something wrong which needs to be addressed. As a society, we have been conditioned to resist and block out what doesn't feel good. But what we haven't been taught is that the ability to feel all depths of emotion is innate within us, and we are fully capable of it. Feeling our emotions is our greatest power, and when we activate and tap into it, this can lead to our greatest healing and transformation. Once an emotion has been suppressed on a body level, you cannot get it out of the body unless you know how.

A very powerful and fast way to heal and release pain in the body is to go deeply into the emotion that we are experiencing and deeply feel it out without suppressing it. This may begin with rage and then shift to sadness; thus begins the grieving and release process.

Another way to heal pain and trauma stored in the body is through simultaneous orgasm and positive affirmations. When we are in orgasm, we are literally in a state of ebb, which is an important aspect of the Divine Feminine. In this space, we can reprogram our identity. All we have to do is to repeat a positive affirmation to ourselves, such as "I am ready to receive love" or "I am worthy" at the very same time we are experiencing an orgasm. This will help us to begin making a shift.

Our sexual energy is our life force energy and when we tap into this level of consciousness, we have the ability to heal the deepest of wounds and manifest our desires at rapid speed. The process of healing shouldn't be focused only on what we wish to release from our bodies and life; it is also important to focus on what we wish to manifest and create. Otherwise we end up in a downward spiral of focusing only on what doesn't feel good rather than focusing more on what does feel good. There needs to be a balance. Creating space in the mind and body by releasing pain, wounds, and old mindsets will create the energetic space within our being to begin manifesting more of what we want and to live a beautiful life.

When the body is given permission to feel pleasure and live in pleasure, a woman will begin to vibrate differently. When we shift our mindset to one that focuses more on what we want rather than what we don't want, we begin to attract different experiences, opportunities, and people into our lives.

Having our mind operating on the same frequency as our body is important for us to stay in alignment with ourselves, our feelings, and our own truth. A person will know when they are caught up in their mind because they will feel numb in their body, too afraid to feel, and unable to get present with themselves and their emotions.

Using orgasm to heal and having a strong mindset is so powerful. This practice has had the most profound impact on my life. It has allowed me to deeply heal the wounds stored at my body level. It has assisted me to birth a new identity and reality for myself and given me the inner freedom that I have always longed for. Freedom to be myself, to not carry any pain, and to live the most expressed and rich life as a woman, mother, wife, and entrepreneur. I can now serve others deeply because I know how to serve myself first. Manifestation time is now shortened because there is nothing in my body telling me, "Eleni, you aren't worthy." The trauma and pain have been cleared. I have stopped striving and am purely living simply by being my true self. I trust myself so deeply and love myself fiercely. I know that the Universe will support me, because I know that *I* am the Universe.

One of the greatest gifts that a woman can commit to is loving and embracing her own sexual powers, appreciating her body, and raising her consciousness. When a woman is able to send love from her heart space to her vagina, she nourishes the Divine Feminine within and is able to create magic from this space. *This* is self-love and self-nourishment. *This* is how a woman can literally birth herself into a new reality and create whatever it is that she chooses through her womb space instead of forcing things to come to her. There is absolutely no need to force anything in life when your mind is clear, your intuition is open, your body is free, and your soul is flourishing. We are living in a time when the Wild Feminine is leading the way for deep healing to occur within all of our relationships. She is the doorway to our freedom, and she is showing us all our way back Home to ourselves, reminding us that we are nothing but pure Divine Love. It is time to rise, dear Sisters, for when one of us rises, we give our other sisters permission to rise as well.

From my heart to yours, Eleni

# SHE IS MEANT TO RECEIVE.

---

# CHAPTER 06

# THE INFINITE AND THE UNKNOWN: YOUR WILD BIRTHRIGHT

BY: HEATHER ALLISON

*"There's a reason it's felt harder than it's supposed to; why it's felt like something's missing. You've only been given half the story, and there is so much MORE meant for you."*

# HEATHER ALLISON

~~~~~~~~~~~~~~~~~~~~~~~~~~~

fb biz: @heatherallisongoldengoddess
fb personal: @agirlcalledbruce
www.heather-allison.com

Heather Allison has been described as a beacon of light and love in the world, sharing her passion and her teachings to help women find the Gold and the Goddess within through coaching, courses, retreats, and books. Her teachings center on bringing an ancient, forgotten, Cosmic Feminine Wisdom and medicine to the world, changing the foundation we build our lives upon and helping women reconnect with their limitlessness, their power, Love, and deep abundance of magic. She helps women reclaim the More they're truly meant for — deep joy, love, success, and rich, intuitive lives. She calls this your Golden Path — and it's there within, simply waiting for you to Remember.

*Goddess, your wildness is everything you think it is,
and nothing you expect it to be.*

*Yours is a Limitlessness that defies conventional
understanding,*

*earthly confines, and conditioned belief.*

*Within you is the Remembrance of a Power, a
Magic, a Love, and a Wildness
that you've never been given permission to know.*

*And it is that which aches within you now;
that you feel stirring and growing and asking to
be released;*

*that is calling you to Remember:*

*You are meant for MORE.*

You've only been given half the story.

**M**y love, your Feminine Wild is even deeper and bigger than you've been allowed to explore.

As we are called more and more to Remember the Divine Feminine power within us, we've been dropping into sacred ceremonies, connecting with our inner Truths, with the depths and darkness of our wombs. We've been committing to feeling everything more deeply, to moving in flow with the tides, to rising and stepping into our light and our grace, as we've always been meant to. And it's beautiful. It's powerful. But it's still only half the story.

What we haven't been given permission to Remember is the Infinite Power we have available to us. We haven't been allowed to believe what we're really capable of, to know who we truly are, to feel the embodied pulse of the Universe, the Divine, the Cosmos, the All That Is, coursing through our bodies. We still embody centuries of conditioning, threads of ancient Wounding, that have blocked us from our true channel and our ability to receive what we're meant for.

This has tricked us into believing, somehow, that we could ever be too much or not enough — opposite sides of the same wound that make us doubt our power, our magic, our limitlessness. We were *built* specifically to receive the Infinite, the vastness of the Universe — and to bring it through into form, to manifest it here.

This isn't a metaphor or hyperbole. This is your actual, foundational Truth as the embodiment of the Cosmic Divine Feminine archetype. When you Remember that she lies within you, ready to bring you back to your deepest knowing and your greatest power, your Destiny will become manifest.

This Cosmic Feminine Archetype is the original blueprint that exists in your cells, in your bones, in your belly, asking to be awakened and activated now.

It is in connecting to exactly this power, to Her, to your deepest, deepest Truth of who you are, that you will uncover the key to your wildest Feminine fulfillment.

This is the Archetypal truth that is asking to be awakened within all of us right now. The Feminine and Masculine Archetypes live within our psyches, our emotions, our thoughts, our dreams, and our bodies, regardless of time, place, culture, or conscious awareness. They tend to steer our actions, reactions, and beliefs more than we ever realize. We've collectively spent thousands and thousands of years burying, forgetting, rejecting, even vilifying the Divine Feminine Archetype. Instead we have been conditioned to value and uphold the Masculine. We have, as a planet and a species, found ourselves dangerously out of balance, living in a starkly Wounded Masculine world paradigm: the damaging patriarchy in which the Masculine Archetype continues to run rampant, unbalanced, unchecked, doubling in on itself with its own re-wounding.

You can see this everywhere around you. It's in the news, in the disregard for and destruction of our planet, in the disconnection from one another, and in the crumbling state of our relationships. You can feel it in the repeating cycles and patterns of pain and struggle that you experience. It is this imbalance and the Wounded Masculine paradigm that is the reason behind our state of suffering in every part of our lives.

It is the reason we have forgotten what we are really capable of and the magic we have access to. It is the reason our relationships fall apart. It is the reason we are so disconnected with the planet, with our bodies, with our intuition, with one another, with ourselves, and with our ability to create the lives we know we're meant for.

It is the reason everything feels harder than it should. It is why we feel something deeply important is missing. And it is exactly why we feel a near-primal craving for a return to our Wildness.

This Wildness as we've been experiencing and exploring thus far has still, unfortunately, been wrapped in the conditioning of the Wounded Masculine paradigm. While we seek the return of the Divine Feminine, our attempts at our re-finding Her and re-finding our Wildness remain tangled with the core belief system that says we're not enough. It keeps us limited by the Patriarchal understanding of who we are, what is possible for us, what we're capable of, and what we're meant for. Without access to the WHOLE Archetypal Truth of who we are, we will continue to be dragged back into the Wound.

But there's more. You are meant for *so* much more.

**And in order to tap into who you truly are and what you're truly meant for**

**— your Wildness —**

**it's necessary to go to the source.**

When you came here, into this lifetime, you were seeded with the possibility and the purpose your Soul chose for your time here. Yet, as happens to all of us, in order to grow to the fullest potential, from our vulnerable infancy, we have to conform to the methods, rules, and agreements of the time and place we grow up in. We have to take on the survival approach that comes with the particular family and cultural dynamics we're born into in order to grow strong and old enough to leave them. We must actually forget why our Soul came here for a while, so that we can choose to fulfill our Purpose later.

Unfortunately, we are also — at least for the time being — born into a time when we're no longer taught how to Remember and step into that purpose when we're finally capable of choosing it. The world as it is now doesn't give us the tools to come back to that Soul seed and the fullness of the possibility we were meant for.

This is why many people are unfulfilled and unsure of what they're supposed to do with their lives, how to find love, who they're supposed to be. It's why so many of us feel lost or feel that we've lost a vital part of ourselves somewhere along the way. We simply assume it's an unavoidable part of life.

But our Souls are still here, breathing within us, sending nudges, whispers, messages, albeit faint and weakened ones from decades of not listening. All it takes to come back to our truest selves, our most vital sparks and exactly what we're meant for, is letting ourselves listen to Her once again.

In order to do that, we have to shake the conditioning, the domestication, the learned behaviors, and beliefs, and come back into our Truth, our Soul-alignment, our Feminine Wildness.

But there's a catch. The fullness of our Feminine Wildness and truest joy cannot be found just by exploring the well-trodden ceremony and ritual; the age-old Feminine practices that are so beautifully being unearthed. While there is a deeply important aspect of Her found there, and it comes with a deep well of collective Remembrance about who we are as a community, as healers, as sisters, mothers, daughters, teachers, lovers — we cannot find her wholeness there exactly *because* it is age-old and well-trodden.

In other words, our Wildness isn't found in what has already been established, what is tried and true, no matter how beautiful, necessary and nourishing it may be.

**The wildest we can be is letting ourselves be blindly guided by our Souls**

**into the Unknown of who we have yet to become.**

I was as stuck in the Wounded Masculine "cage" as anyone else before I found this work, and I didn't even know it. Until the age of thirty-nine, I'd spent my entire life living what I call an "almost life." Almost happy, almost fulfilled, almost the right guy, almost the right job . . . but never quite. I bounced from relationship to relationship, job to job, thinking I'd found "the one," only to have my heart broken or my hopes dashed again and again. Every single time, there was some unnameable, unknowable thing that just didn't feel like me. And I didn't know how to find the thing that did.

But we always know when there's something missing. When it feels "not quite." When it feels "almost." We can sense when there's supposed to be more, when it's supposed to be easier. I could feel it, I could almost taste it, it felt so close. Yet I couldn't quite see what it was supposed to look like, let alone how to get there.

I didn't know what I would eventually uncover when I stumbled upon the thread of the Divine Feminine. I didn't know that, within eight months, I would have the most profound spiritual awakening because of Her, and that my previous "almost happy" life would be unrecognizable to me a few short months later. With that spiritual awakening, I began to receive intuitive information about the archetypes, their energies, and the quantum mechanics of how they work within our lives, our relationships, and psyches, as well as how to teach this to others.

I've seen the most mind-blowing transformation in the women I've taught this to. Through healing and re-patterning their Archetypal foundation and connecting them to the Energetic Blueprint they were built for, women find themselves. They find the love they've been missing, their purpose, and a profound connection with their Soul.

One of the most important things my clients come to understand is that the things they seek to do, the dreams they wish to fulfill, the love they desire to feel, doesn't come from applying a template, nor does it come from any of the ways they've been previously shown. Instead, it comes from connecting with their own unique Blueprint, their truest paths, the voice of their Souls, and allowing themselves to be guided to exactly what they are meant for. Their freedom, their Feminine Wildness, is uncovered by peeling away the limitations, the should's, and the assumed and stepping to the edge where Known and Unknown meet and begin to co-create with Infinite Possibility. Our Wildness is that which cannot be tamed, possessed, planned, or plotted on any spreadsheet. It cannot be bound by any lines. And so it is when we learn to no longer look outside of ourselves for our direction and instead come inside, to a clear and profound dialogue with our Soul: this is when we find our Wildness.

**Our Soul is where we find our Wildness.**

**And it is there that we finally come Home.**

The truth is this: Our Soul knows more than us. She's the one who decided to come here, to this life, to this body, to this version of You. She's the one who knows the path you're meant to walk, and exactly how to reach the things that are meant for you. And She has a much bigger plan for us than we do.

When we release ourselves from the expectations of what we should be doing and instead allow ourselves to be shown, we will be guided on a journey we never expected, and one we could never have imagined.

Here's why:

For as much as we practice accessing our earthy Feminine energy, and as necessary as that is, if we're not bringing in both the human, earthy Feminine energy and our other, higher Feminine aspect — the Soul — and embodying Her as fully as possible, we are only working with a part of our blueprint, a fragment of our intended abilities, experiences, and gifts. We are only receiving a fraction of what is meant to come to us. We're only accessing one aspect of who we are.

When we allow ourselves to embody the duality and become both the rich, dark, fertile soil of the Earthy Feminine *and* the mysterious, paradoxical and untamable Cosmic Feminine — when we become the fullness of the Divine Feminine in her dual nature — we become the vessel to receive Divine wisdom, deep understanding, and higher consciousness. We receive the abundant gifts of the Universe. We receive the beauty and the Love we're built for.

In other words, when we are fully our Feminine selves — body and Soul, manifest and celestial — we are capable of co-creating with the Universe and can then receive exactly what we're meant for, in every aspect of our lives.

## How to Apply our Wildness

To start listening more deeply to your fullest, Wildest Feminine self, there are a few transformative practices.

The first is this: Throw away the template. Whatever has been handed to you, ingrained in you, or taught to you, allow yourself to create at least the possibility for its rewiring. Flirt with the idea that there's more to life, more to you, and more to what's possible for you than just this. Allow for there to be another way that you might not yet know, that you might not yet have been shown. The more you allow yourself to tap into and embrace the Unknown, the more you connect to the realm where your Soul resides. She will always be calling you into what is beyond "What Is" and into your Limitlessness.

Secondly, create the conditions that are ripest for hearing your Soul. Make time for a morning practice that includes meditation in which you simply ask, "What would you like me to know today?" and then listen. Pay attention to your dreams. Write them down, as much as you can remember, and take time to see what they might be telling you. Listen to your body. She knows so much more than we give Her credit for. The next time you're making a decision, check in with what She has to say. Does she get tight, tense, heavy, resistant? Or does she feel lighter, freer, more open, more alive? Stop talking yourself out of your Soul nudges. I know that sometimes the things She is asking of us don't seem to make sense. But when did we start believing that we know better than our Souls?

Thirdly: Start taking brazen action in honor of Her. This is sometimes the hardest part. We must at least take baby steps in service of honoring the whispers that come from deep within. Remember, we are the physical manifestation of our Souls. We are Her representative here in this physical plane. If we're not taking action toward what She's calling us into, who will? Who will create the life, the success, the Love, the magic that we are meant for, if not you?

You are the one who pulls the strings, shifts the gears, puts one physical foot in front of the other. And She will be there, within you, at your side, whispering, nudging, calling you forward, and orchestrating timing, "coincidences," meetings, and magic as you go.

When you give your Soul a big enough Channel by following these suggestions, She will do all the work for you. And life will begin to flow in ways you couldn't possibly imagine . . . but She can.

And the last thing, beautiful, that I want to leave with you is this:

Remember, Wild one, that you are Limitless.

That your Wildness is found in the Infinite expanse of what's Possible for you.

That you are deeply Loved, deeply guided, and profoundly capable.

Remember that there is SO MUCH MORE available to you —
— and that much of it exists in the realm of the invisible . . .

NURTURE BY

ACCEPTING

EVERYONE'S

UNIQUE BEING.

# CHAPTER 07

# GODDESS LILITH:

# FACE OF THE WILD FEMININE

## BY: MOLLIE LYDDANE

*"Lilith is the fire of the feminine that will serve to restore balance and equality to this planet, a goddess long suppressed in the collective psyche and ordained for wide-scale emergence."*

# DR. MOLLIE LYDDANE

www.drlyddane.com

Mollie harbored a glimmering suspicion she would become a psychologist during high school, when the paradoxes and complexities of the human condition became a strong subject of curiosity and investigation through her interests in philosophy and literature.

During her college years, she became mesmerized with the study of astrology as a way of discovering how different people filter and organize their experience. Later studies in hypnotherapy led Mollie to dive wholeheartedly into the world of clinical psychology with the purpose of exploring the dynamics of psychotherapy, human emotional connection, and psychological intimacy. Jungian therapy, psychodynamic therapy, humanistic therapy, and mindfulness serve to inform her approach to psychotherapeutic encounter. Spiritual pursuits in meditation and yoga are foundational to Mollie's life. Her creativity takes many forms through dance, writing, and archetypal imagery. She considers herself an eternal student, mystic, and explorer of life's underground mysteries. Today Mollie works in the San Francisco Bay Area as a clinical psychologist and astrologer. Her Persian kitten, Merlin, serves as a perpetual reminder of play as an aspect of our essential nature as humans.

*"So what compromises the Wild Woman?
From the viewpoint of archetypal psychology
as well as in ancient traditions, she is the
female soul. Yes she is more; she is the
source of the feminine. She is all that is of
instinct, of the worlds both seen and hidden
- she is the basis. We each receive from her
a glowing cell which contains all the instincts
and knowing needed for our lives."*
~ Clarissa Pinkola Estes

I am still learning the ways of the Wild Woman. Every new day is a dip in the stream of this river of wild of being. It is the nature of me: I seek to discover and reveal with so much desperation that I give my life to Her. I aim for careful attention in the listening and responding to this instinct, this life impulse.

She feels much like an outlier, an electric current, a spontaneous arising that leans toward that otherly realm and forever seeks the beyond. In me, there is Lilith, the dark Goddess in whom I find much of my "wild" knowing. There is a felt-sense of her presence and her protection. This chapter is devoted to those who recognize Lilith as an intrinsic aspect of their own personal psychology.

It is difficult to note when I first identified and isolated Lilith in name as a figure to behold. She has surfaced many times throughout the course of my life, to reflect her values of equality, independence, and authenticity. Perhaps most vividly in my recollection, she surfaced in name during the first year of my own personal psychotherapy. Personal psychotherapy was a requirement as a budding psychologist in training. I was drawn toward working with a depth psychologist who favored a Jungian orientation and was well-versed in mythology and symbols and the ways dreams operated to reflect deeper levels of meaning in our life experience.

## The Scold's Bridle

Very early on in our work together, my analyst pointed me to an image of a mask designed for women in the sixteenth and seventeenth centuries: the scold's bridle. Women were forced to wear it as a form of public humiliation. Women suspected of witchcraft and considered by their husbands to be "nags" would be punished through means of this mask. Husbands were not questioned in their decision to humiliate their wives, as their power in the marriage was also without question. Husbands would parade their wives, wearing the bridle, around town to showcase the women's "unruly" behavior and "loose" tongues. Many of these masks made speaking impossible due to the sharp spikes that would press down upon the tongue or from underneath the mouthpiece. Some of these bridles had mouthpieces that made it difficult to swallow and metal pieces on the sides of the ears, so that passersby would be able to pound loud drum noises into the wearer's ears.

There was often a chain tied to the mask, for the husband to use while he paraded his wife about town. Being led through a walk of shame was an experience that no woman would soon forget. It was something I had not been taught in school, and certainly not something that surfaced in mainstream texts. In my years of being a psychotherapist, very few clients have been aware of these masks, which reflect the barbaric practices of a polite society and how grossly distorted mass perception can become. The people of this time and place enforced these inhumane, grotesque practices upon women routinely and without question.

What do you imagine it would be like, to be dragged through the streets donning this mask and to see the onlookers sneering at and condemning you? How would it be to feel the embarrassment and the shame? How might you feel about your husband, who is leading you through town like cattle?

Can you imagine being a female onlooker, subject to this conditioning agent as a powerful force in controlling your mannerisms and behaviors? It would be a natural and expected response to feel a sense of betrayal, confusion, and deep anger as you watch the freedom that is slipping through your fingers, as your life becomes molded and curtailed to suit the absurd laws of the land. Proceeding with semi-paralysis would likely register as safe practice with which to move through the world as a woman.

These practices were not so long ago. These experiences are burned deeply into the collective female psyche, and are that which we are committed to healing. Lilith's story becomes re-claimed through more conscious awareness of true histories of women being shamed and treated like livestock, subject to the whimsical punishment of their husbands, and unjustly dehuman-ized by a patriarchal society. These are the stories that light Lilith's fire. The lifeblood of these pained realities lies not in the mere lighting of the fire, the fuller awareness of how the female voice has been suppressed, but also in the protection of the steady flame of remembering and hearing this voice of the Wild Feminine. The process of reclaiming her essential thunder is ongoing.

## Lilith

Originally a sacred Sumerian priestess, Lilith arises as a complex archetypal figure. Those who have gone before in an attempt to define her draw upon images from the Old Testament, the Kabbal-ah, pagan myth, and European fairy tale. In Hebrew legend, Lilith represented the original wife of Adam in the Genesis story of the Garden of Eden. Made of the same intrinsic material of Adam, she insisted on equality. Her refusal to play subservient to Adam gen-erated a great deal of controversy and negative press as a result. Stories differ on whether she fled the Garden of Eden or whether she was cast out; ultimately, it is of no matter either way.

Lilith reminds us that a land void of gender equality is no paradise at all. Her story is the tale of a woman who knows her value and will not permit herself to be defined or treated as less. She carries herself with dignity and a fiery autonomous disposition. As a col-lectively repressed and suppressed aspect of the human psyche, she is increasingly being called to the forefront of our awareness, to be owned and integrated into a fuller expression of wholeness. She is a face of the Wild Feminine that seeks to be seen and heard with increasing urgency.

## Lilith in Relationships

Lilith calls for respect. She is certain and clear as to her worth. She is not always so clear or certain, however, as to whether others can deliver the level of respect that she seeks. Expectations in relationships need to be articulated clearly to avoid unnecessary confusion and the resulting dissolution of trust. I have been in situations more than once wherein she has surfaced rather dramatically as a result of the vague ambiguities that colored the parameters of my romantic involvements.

There is a great deal of emotional upheaval when Lilith perceives herself as being taken for granted or at risk of having the rug pulled out from under her. And even when expectations and boundaries are set, shit happens. I recall quite vividly the intensity of rage coursing through my body upon discovery that a past partner was cheating on me and betraying my trust. The dreamscape became my safe place for Lilith to roam, and breathe, and express herself; in this space, I lit many a bonfire of his most cherished pieces of art, mostly ones he had made for me.

Under Lilith's directive, I burned them all to the ground in a grand celebratory symbolic gesture in my mind, serving as ceremonial tribute to the rage I was due and as a representation of the deeper transmutation process at work.

Lilith is not Eve, and she never will be. Subservience is not her nature. She is best met by a partner who appreciates her strength, her authority over herself, and her tenacious pursuit of freedom. She seeks an equal and someone who will find an equal in her. Lilith craves honesty in union, a kind of raw honesty that asks for courage. To relate at this level can be terrifying. She needs someone who seeks to understand her and lean in to hear her inner rumblings. She is met by someone who honors her emotionality and can hold steady. She needs someone who can acknowledge her rage rather than fleeing from it.

Lilith's growth edge is ensuring that rage is felt, expressed safely, and with care. She runs on electricity that is both wholly intoxicating and difficult to manage. She does not care for rules and expectations if they are assigned to her, but she can work with them if there is mutuality in their creation. Traditional men following traditional modes of thinking about a "woman's place" will find her troublesome and difficult.

So be it. They are not for her.

## Lilith in Her Sovereignty

It is Lilith's prerogative to lead a single life that does not make man or "other" the center of it. There are periodic times of chosen exile for Lilith: time in solitude, when she seeks renewal from the mundane and a return to herself. She will not lose sight of who she is and what is important. She recognizes the compromises involved in a relationship and holds to her backbone, her will.

I find her in solitude, something I seek out and revel in frequently when excessive relating and over-extension threaten a great disconnect within myself. Time alone allows me to remember to listen and to respond to the needs and desires that arise and fall, of myself as giver and receiver of this cycle. Her offering is to listen to the echoes of our ancestry, our collective wounding, and our collective aspirational drives.

Lilith asks us to reconnect to what we stand for and what we find of value, based not on the whimsical trends of society but in what rings true from that deep reservoir of knowledge. Lilith reminds us of what it feels like to be a free, autonomous woman whose soul yearnings can finally be heard, whose purpose cannot be traded within the transactional affairs of relationship. Lilith offers us the opportunity to bask in the stillness and the quiet of our human experience, so that we may finally settle in and hear her.

## Lilith in the Workplace

Lilith works with others when mutual respect is an implicit and shared value. It is worth reiterating that in every area of her life, this will be true. This tends to equate most often to difficulty being bossed around, particularly with any degree of reckless disregard. Lilith has arisen rather dramatically within me when authority has attempted to wield power over me in any kind of demonstrative show. Lilith does not play well in that charade. She does her best work as a self-employed entity or where a tremendous amount of freedom is offered. This is largely because she does not have to gratify bosses or reach for metaphorical "carrots" being dangled before her.

Several years ago, I worked for a company whose director stormed into my private space one afternoon in an exaggerated and unnecessary display of power. In pure Lilith fashion, I left that very afternoon and never came back. The event prompted a necessary discourse with my analyst about how I could work with Lilith energy to hold true to her ways.

Lilith's need for respect may be considered admirable in some places, but as an employee, she has a hard time letting prideful individuals in places of greater authority oversee or threaten her freedom and sovereignty. Understanding her is a necessary step in ensuring her assets are highlighted. She is most assuredly a leader who does not care to grovel.

## Lilith as a Guiding Principle

Lilith's way is the way out of the Garden of Eden. Though story may speak of her fleeing the Garden of Eden, my experience of her declares that the Garden of Eden was never her home. The Garden of Eden has a kind of matrix-like reality of its own, governed by a patriarchal paradigm that would suffocate her. She lives in all of us to some extent, male or female, and yet she does live more consciously and openly in the psychology of individuals to varying degrees. Lilith's path is unscripted.

Though often deeply misunderstood, she is also brave enough to bear the burden of living a life that many people will question. Acknowledging her role in my life and giving her more opportunity for expression gives me the chance to learn how to honor her as an internalized figure of wisdom. Lilith has a voice that will be heard by those ready to receive her. She calls for the Wild in women to rise to the surface. *"There is no coming to consciousness without pain,"* as Carl Jung is quoted as saying. Anger that arises from acknowledging deeply buried truths is a necessary pain if there is to be a more truthful interface with who we are.

We need to understand what we have endured collectively in order to reclaim what has been lost. We remember the reality of the scold's bridle to remember a piece of the collective female wound that we are actively, consciously working to mend. We remember to ensure that atrocities such as the scold's bridle do not repeat.

It would be an error to believe we are not still effectively wearing these masks, as the psychological underpinnings are still deeply entrenched in the feminine. Removing them requires conscious attention and intention to practice, day by day. In this way, this book of the Wild Feminine is one small step in response to this call: a call that will repeat for as long as necessary to effect the necessary healing of the feminine wound.

Lilith calls for us to remember who we are intrinsically as women, at our core, beyond the roles we step into for others. Coming into a stronger sense of Lilith consciousness brings us into closer contact with the foundation of our lives, our wild essence, and our own moral authority. She is spontaneous, uncontrived, and always expressing her deep hunger for what is true in this life. Her beauty resides in her uncompromising nature, where one's essential and honest expression is given room to breathe.

Her deliberate intention is to respond to the elemental aspects of our being and to lead a life of her own design. At this point in our history, Lilith seeks to be integrated more consciously into our lives, to equalize the genders, and to bring more purpose and joy to our life experience. It is our very destiny to let her in and honor our Wild Feminine.

WE SAW WOMEN STRIVING TO FIND THEIR POSITION OF POWER BY ABANDONING THEIR FEMININE ENERGY. AMY MERAKI

---

# CHAPTER 08

# WE ALWAYS GET A CHOICE

## BY: MICHELLE ARNOLD

*"Living in shame means living in another person's path, you can always chose to make your own path."*

# MICHELLE ARNOLD

ig: @JustMichelleArnold

Michelle Arnold has been a medical laboratory technician, spiritual coach, speaker, writer, and philosophy major. She has had a strong connection and love for the metaphysical world since her first college course focused on The Law of Attraction and Quantum Physics. She brings her wisdom and philosophies to those around her daily. Michelle is a leader amongst her family, friends, co-workers, and clients for bringing her unique perspective and vibrant and positive energy to all of life's offerings.

Among Michelle's many creative outlets, such as traveling, writing, dancing, and playing the piano, you can find her channeling her creativity by creating healing dream catchers, which she ships around the world. Her grandfather taught her how to make them as a child and she has found ways to enhance them with natural healing crystals and energy.

I grew up on a dead-end road with a large field and pond in my backyard. If I could stay outside all day to bury my head in the lilac bushes, brush the vines of the weeping willows with my fingers, and lay with the geese, it was a good day. We had a large rock in the middle of the yard that I believed was made just for me to sit perfectly on and stare at the clouds. Those were the days when I knew nothing yet everything.

Even though today I can openly share my story with you, it wasn't always this way. I've spent many years hiding pieces of it that I was ashamed to share.

I was about nineteen years old when I testified against my father in federal court. I can still feel the unbearable pain as I was asked to identify him across the courtroom. The kind of pain that makes your eyes and every muscle in your face burn as you feel a lump in your throat that gets in the way of you swallowing down any ounce of life left in your body.

As I sat on the witness stand, a flood of emotions came over me. To my surprise, anger was the least felt; realizing that anger was *not* in the driver's seat actually *made* me angry. I was hurt, I felt abandoned, misunderstood, humiliated, shamed, judged: why the hell wasn't I angry? I thought being angry would make the whole situation more digestible. Instead, I was reminiscing about a time my father and I laughed so hard we cried, jammin' to Elvis and giving butterfly kisses.

My father spent most of my childhood in prison. I would go to visit him and we would sit and talk, take Polaroid photos at the photo booth, and eat vending machine snacks. I remember that everyone enjoyed his company and the officers were always so fond of him. He was (and I believe still is) so much fun to be around. He's always been someone to light up a room with his personality. I would be so excited to see him and I enjoyed spending time with him; we were always alike in so many ways.

When it was time to leave, it was back to reality and everyday life: not speaking of my father *or* the time we spent together. Growing up, I believed that having a criminal in the family was something to keep quiet. I felt that somehow mentioning my father or our time together would portray my family and me like something other than what we were. I just knew we didn't discuss this; it was looked down upon and something to be ashamed of.

Ever since I could remember, I had this feeling of *hope*: a feeling that maybe my father never had the *opportunity* to become someone different, someone I trusted and could depend on. Maybe it was just an excuse I told myself to help me feel better throughout the years and avoid accepting that he never chose me. Either way, I needed to learn all of it for myself.

I began spending more time with my father around the age of eighteen (roughly a year before he was arrested again). I hoped somehow we would be able to make up for all of the years we missed out on each other. I started to disconnect with my family because I felt they would be ashamed of me for choosing to see him, let alone let him live with me. It was familiar for me to want to hide and be ashamed of myself, but I was curious about my father, and I missed the feeling (or *idea*) of being his daughter. We did have a lot of fun together, but I began to see things play out as my family had always warned me. I felt angry at myself for not listening to the people who cared about me — they seemed to know better. It wasn't long before I noticed a loaded gun on my kitchen table, crack cocaine in my car, random women coming around, and then it was the gun pointed at me as a joke. Not a funny one. I didn't want to believe any of it. When they say love is blind, sometimes it's really fucking blind.

I was a witness to several criminal charges that would put my father away *again* for what ended up being twenty-one years. I woke up one morning to the ATF (Alcohol Tobacco and Firearms) at the front door. I thought of sneaking out of the basement window and running, but the only way out would put me in the driveway in plain sight of the ATF. So instead, the officers and I sat at the kitchen table where I was told that they wanted my father for breaking parole and needed proof of him with a gun. (Insert nervous laughter.) Essentially, they needed my help making his arrest and then testifying in front of a grand jury if his case made it to trial . . . which it did. I thought to myself, "This is *my dad*, and everyone will find out about this. Maybe people will think I can't be trusted or that I'm a bad person for wanting to spend time with a criminal." I started making up these stories in my mind of what people would think.

I don't know his story, and it's not mine to understand. However, I can tell you why it happened for me. I never wanted to accept any of this. If I did, that meant it was real. I would have rather stayed in the shame because it was familiar and meant that there was still hope for a different ending. But none of that way of living ever felt like home for me. Living in that shame meant that I was living a life for someone else's path. It was time to make my own. Stating my name to the jury meant that I was choosing me. I was choosing to accept my path and my experience exactly as is and saying thank you and goodbye to all that I knew.

*You get a choice, Wild Woman. You can continue to bury your head in the sand like the Ostrich, as Grandma would say, or you can speak up, own your story, and set forth as a Wild Woman, knowing that all life passes and happens FOR you, not to you. Take these choices and share them. Feel them. Accept them. Speak them.*

"Can you please state your name for the Jury?"

Inhale. Exhale. "Michelle Arnold."

THE FEMININE STILLNESS
CAN BE ISOLATING.

GREATER YIN CAN BE BALANCED
THROUGH ACTS OF SELF-LOVE.

# CHAPTER 09

# I'M DEAD INSIDE – NOW WHAT?

## BY: S.C. VOLLMER

*"Healing comes in many forms and often from unsuspecting places. There's a phoenix in each of us — we can always be reborn."*

# S.C. VOLLMER

~~~~~~~~~~~~~~~~~~~~~

t: @fARfROMLuCK | in: @kitt-kat
www.researchgate.net/profile/S_Vollmer

S.C. Vollmer can usually be found with either her head in the clouds or a glassy, distant look in her eyes. "I'm thinking," is her only source of nutrition. After traveling coast-to-coast in Canada and starting and stopping more businesses than she cares to admit (does having a "5pm lemonade stand outside a bus stop" as a seven-year-old count?), she has decided that, yes, multi-colored LED backlights on keyboards were worth it. With almost more degrees than one can count with their (one) hand, she has confirmed that being paid to think is so far the best thing that's happened yet. And so, after promising to get a "real job," she now spends most of her time *back* in academia, fusing software engineering and painting, coding (playing) in Virtual Reality, creating artistic "scapes," and envisioning the future of how the world could be. Kinesthetically speaking, proprioception is the best.

*When I look inside and see that I am nothing, that is wisdom*

*When I look outside and see that I am everything, that is love.*

*And between these two, my life turns.*

~ Sri Nisargadatta Maharaj

**W**hen I think of what kind of person I might be, I am usually split between multiple worlds and trains of thought. I often consider myself to live with one foot in, one foot out, regardless of the situation.

I was re-inspired to write this chapter after an event I attended at one of the Royal Ontario Museum's "ROM Speaks" nights. It was an evening of discussion over an exhibit of Philip Beesley and Iris Van Herpen, who came together along with filmmaker Stylianos Pangalos to discuss their fusion of art and science into a fascinating display of architectural artistry and reflection-based futuristic fashion (my words, not theirs).

During the evening, I kept noticing this growing tapestry of interwoven threads of competing ideals, this notion that there are often boundaries between art and science and yet,

when they collide,

we find ourselves at the forefront of discovery.

Of intuition.

Of untethered curiosity.

This same night, a couple of new colleagues and I were wandering (but not lost!) through the streets of Toronto. One of them turned to me and exclaimed that it was interesting to be around me because I made people feel happier than they are. I thought this was a curious way of describing someone. I thought about what she said later that night and I realized that it wasn't the first time someone has pointed out the emotional influence I have on others. Right now, a few days later, I am still sitting here, wondering if that feeling I elicit in others is because I am genuinely invested in every individual I interact with or if it has more to do with my open and curious nature. Perhaps instead, it has everything to do with my depth of consideration and understanding of what I feel are ethereal eternal balances in life. To know beauty is, perhaps, to also know pain.

I don't particularly think I am conscious of the way I interact with others. It is more fluid, more intuitive. It surges from within, and I see what I want to see in others. I see what is there, beneath the surface. Occasionally, this proves difficult. It's not for nothing that there is an entire discipline of research on personality and cognition, which is often motivated (I am sure!) because of the difficulties in connecting and communicating with human persons who are significantly different in outlook and values than ourselves.

I am referring more to the innate cognition and preferences of individuals, which is not cultural or location-specific. Rather, it transcends these divisions and speaks to the various ways in which humans have evolved to interact with themselves and others.

When we are confronted with individuals with whom we think we have not much in common and communication is difficult, it is certainly a challenge to develop anything more than, at best, a cordial, superficial relationship. Even *that* is, at times, seemingly awkward and useless to some. I engender compassion and an empathetic mirror. I see your pain through your forced smile, and I wonder if you can see mine. I had a conversation with a close friend of mine just the other day, and I surprised him with an unusual bout of honest personal revelations. He was quite surprised at some of the thoughts I expressed having. I was deep into a twisted mental dive, curiously debating with myself about the point of continued existence if one felt they had already lived enough to last a lifetime.

If humans are archetypically driven by curiosity, is there a point at which the old adage "there's nothing new under the sun" feels real? And if so, why is there so much pressure to live your life *as long as you can*, with significantly less emphasis globally on providing a superior quality of life? Why do we prefer someone keeps their life, but we don't reach out enough to others to ensure that their life is recognized, valued, and loved?

Maybe it's just me, but I find the concept of life and death awkwardly fascinating. I know it's a fact of reality — but what does it mean to be alive? I struggled with this concept at an age that was far too young for my liking. One of my earliest memories is of sitting alone on my bed, bawling my eyes out. Staring at the stars, my heart ached. I was consumed with grief and tormented with accepting myself. I had just found out that I was standing on this thing, Earth, and that it was a "planet" that "was spinning around a ball of fire" and "floating" in this massive expanse of nothing called "space."

I was fascinated with the idea of understanding the world around me (in what I now know to be a "scientific" way) but I had no idea how to reconcile this new ideology. At the time, I only understood it to be incompatible with religion, spirituality, and the safety of my soul. And so I sobbed, hyperventilating and aching until I had nothing left in me. While I was sobbing, I heard a voice. It was not a voice in the sense of someone talking out loud to me. It was more of a knowing. Everything was okay. My child-like logic spoke to me from a deeper well of wisdom. If I existed as I was, if I was created to be who I am, then this was exactly how I was meant to be and my thoughts were valid. There would be no punishment for my curiosity and longing for a duality in my life. Science and spirituality could coexist for me, and it was perfectly acceptable. This was the first time I remember bearing witness to my own soul, shedding my layers, and emerging anew.

This also reminds me of a time, maybe five years or so ago. I was on a crowded bus and I was stuck standing along with a full busload of others. I remember looking around and noticing an individual who was sitting with his head slightly lowered. He had tears streaming down his face. He appeared disheveled and unkempt amongst the backdrop of suited commuters returning from a long day's work. Some people did not notice the tears but made comments on his appearance. I wrestled with my internal thoughts for a few minutes but decided to crouch down and touch his knee. I looked him in the eyes and said, "I know I don't know you, and I know you don't know me, but I just want you to know that no matter what this pain is from, I care that you are hurting and I wish it wasn't happening."

I can remember the next moment so vividly that it still brings a sharp tear to my eyes. In one brief moment, when he looked up and we locked eyes, I saw that his pain had subsided.

"Thank you," he said. "You have no idea how much I needed to hear that. I think I fucked up and I have no idea how to make it right. I haven't been able to sleep and I haven't been to work. I've been on this bus all day. I must look like shit." We talked a bit more after that and his demeanor began to shift into one with a sense of refocused direction and purpose.

"I'm not sure I'll be able to fix what I've done, but yeah, I'll give it a go. Yeah, it'll hurt like fuck if it's not enough but I have the confidence to try now. I'll probably never see you again, but thank you." He jumped up and got off at the next stop.

Now I have *no idea* how his story ends, but one way or another, I think so much came from that single interaction. If it didn't change him, it certainly changed me, as do all of my intense encounters. It certainly changed a number of others on that bus, based on their quizzical and softened expressions, even if for just a short while. I have never wanted to be someone too afraid or too uncomfortable to bridge that lonely gap that divides us. I think a large part of this is because, from an early age, I have confronted the large and lonely gap within myself over and over and over again. I think all of this speaks to the broken heart of our global human connection and our inability to be cared for openly. When people would rather side-eye their neighbor while scoffing at you instead of offering compassion, they erode the very foundation upon which we stand. Ripples of displeasure amplify one another and erupt into crushing waves of dissent. Coursing through society at large, giant riptides of disrespect are pulling us under. It's no wonder that we are drowning in issues such as poor mental health, war, human exploitation, fear, and hate. Perhaps, though, it's a two-way street. Maybe we create situations and then don't know how to handle them.

I suppose this could come down to ownership. If I can't help feeling sad, I would hope that anyone around me (family, coworkers, randoms on a bus) could accept that and not need for me to change. I hope that they would allow me the space to work it out. I also want to accept that if they can't, I wouldn't become defensive. I want to accept that I could understand where they are coming from and that we could work out some agreement. A soul-contract of gracious acceptance and anything that dissipates the hate and reinvigorates.

I want this for anyone, anywhere (even for all us *"Just leave me alone, I am fine!"* types). But there are so many places on this planet where everything I've said here is a dream. My whole chapter, this whole book, is irrelevant if you can't afford a book. It's irrelevant if you're running from your home with nowhere to go. It's irrelevant if you're terrified for your life or do not have the luxury to thrive *because you are still just trying to survive.* If we constantly omit the human factor, then we are quite possibly reinforcing a global human perspective where entire aspects of our humanity are not welcome.

This perplexes me to no end. How radical this world could be if more room was given to idealists, to creatives, to kindness, to conscientiousness, to sustainable progression. How can we progress as a global species which, for all intents and purposes, is alone in this universe, while still maintaining an ideology of the selfish "mine mine mine"? This way of thinking directly limits our potential. I am not afraid to say I am an idealist in all senses of the word. I tend to say this to realists: reality is what we make of it. If I can envision a better world, then one day my idealism will be your reality. At that point, your present realist attitudes and beliefs will have been my past idealisms. There's really no reason for a realist to get in the way of idealism.

Realists are satisfied with what is and not what could be, and so, she says controversially, get out of the way of those that can make what you can't see, be. We're going to do it anyway.

I certainly have an idealistic point of view about what it *could* mean to be alive. Paradoxically, I also have a nihilistic streak of what it means to be alive *right now*. I use this to fuel my fire and at times wallow in an existential mental place.

My own personal yin/yang: I think we can always do better. We can always give more. I use "we" as a global WE, as a constant progression forward for a more humane existence.

I am calling out to anyone who will listen to stand with me (let's be honest — I'll call out even if no one is listening!) to consciously remind themselves every day, to remember the past, to live in the present, and to care for the future. I've always loved the idea of considering your impact not just on yourself and your local community, but on the global stage, and living as if seven generations from now are just as important to you. Do I live perfectly? A thousand times no. In fact, I tell myself to "do as I say, not as I do" rather frequently. Change is often not lasting if it is sudden; rather it's the consistent commitment that will create a lasting impact.

This planet has a long way yet to go. One day of global news illustrates all you need to know: that we need to call upon each other, to open our hearts to a new way of living centered in the acknowledgment of a universal connection between us, one that respects and allows love to flow. To collectively choose to raise the bar of existence on global education standards, living conditions, environmental care, and social structure, and do so with compassion and warmth. Get your hands dirty, covered in the mud of reshaping the world.

To do this, I urge you to be whole, to know yourself, and be one again with your inner voice. Heal yourself so that you can heal others. It is never too late to start over. Believe in second, third, and fourth chances. You don't always have to accept these from others, but it's important to accept them for yourself. It is a powerful thing to be able to burn your light, even if dim, when surrounded by forces that might extinguish you. Pull any and all energy you have access to toward you, moving forward with a wild feminine strength. Look fear in the face and accept that the past shadows may come to haunt you, but stay strong with resolve. You've made the changes necessary for your soul. You know the way. The world should be so lucky to have everyone forgive themselves and grow with wisdom and love, instead of being pulled back down by undesired pain and shadows. Life will find a way. Let it find you.

"Come to the edge," [s]he said.

"We can't, we're afraid!" they responded.

"Come to the edge," [s]he said.

"We can't, We will fall!" they responded.

"Come to the edge," [s]he said.

And so they came.

And [s]he pushed them.

**And they flew.** - Guillaume Apollinaire

HER FEELINGS

ARE HER

SUPERPOWER.

UNLEASHING HER WILD

# CHAPTER 10

# WILDERNESS EMBODIED

## BY: ANGELICA JILL GRACE

*"Giving back authority to the tender and wild animal of my sensual body was the greatest gift I could have ever given myself. It took revering Her as my mentor, friend, and lover to come unabashedly alive with the purposeful ecstasy that dwelled within me all along."*

# ANGELICA JILL GRACE

ig: @sacredinneralchemy | fb: Angelica Jill Grace
e: angelica@sacredinneralchemy.com
www.sacredinneralchemy.com

Angelica Jill Grace is a psychosomatic therapist and sensual embodiment mentor/intimacy coach who supports women, men, and couples who yearn for ultimately fulfilling and empowering intimate connections. She gently guides them in creating sensational and sustainable love lives by coming home to themselves through conscious presence, body love and awareness, and authentic communication.

For as long as I can remember, a grounded inner knowing has lived inside me: sometimes tender, silent, and comforting like a honey-soaked cloak of compassion, other times loud, fiery, and reckless like a fire-spitting dragon. Always, however, relentless in its pursuit to stir me awake to the love of life itself. It is crystal clear, unwavering knowing that I came here for a reason, that my life is to be devoted to the betterment of our species, to the goodness of heart and clarity of conscience that will hopefully contribute to the world having *breathed with just a little more ease* because I lived. It is wild in its desire to remind me that we are forces of nature with the power of a thousand strikes of lightning to usher in a new soulful era of purpose-driven femme leadership.

If you are reading this, chances are you recognize yourself in the essence of this knowing. Perhaps you, too, because of the wild mess that is life, lost touch with the guidance of this knowing somewhere along the way. Perhaps you, too, seemingly lost parts of yourself in traumatic events, borrowed beliefs, and unhealthy relationships. Perhaps our stories mirror each other, interwoven in a similar fabric, or maybe they appear worlds apart. Either way, my innermost wish is for all of us to trace back the steps to our shared core and remember, through the honest expression of what is *real* for us, who we are, why we came here and how we — from a cup that is overflowing — can support each other to *thrive*.

This is our path as wild femme creatures, who go against the grain to create new ways of working, living, collaborating, relating, and being in our communities. Ways that are regenerative, more in harmony with nature around us and within us. We choose to create breakthroughs from breakdowns and with the acquired wisdom leave a legacy to be proud of for centuries to come. A legacy that offers itself as a sacred invitation for future generations to recognize the source and force of life, of nature, and of the power that resides in all sentient beings *as something to be revered and protected*, starting with our very own vessels of flesh and blood — the microcosms in the macrocosm that is Nature. We work for this to be so blatantly obvious that anything else feels utterly and madly ridiculous. Because it is mad to not be in touch with our inner authority, guidance, and compass, to not see our body as a sacred representation of spirit in form.

When we fail to see how very precious and worthy we are, this is directly reflected in our relationship with our body, food, work and money, love, and sex and relationships, as well as in our ability to feel the playful joy for life that naturally resides within us and our capacity to receive love into our longing depths for connection. When we are not allowing this nourishing flow to engulf us, we feel numb, disconnected, and as though we do not belong to this world. No greater threat to humankind or this planet has ever existed. The time is now to use the voices of our wombs and songs of our souls the way they were intended: to have a positive impact that ripples out into the cosmos for love, courage, and an unbridled zest for life to make a home in every willing heart.

I know the language of this inner knowing because I consistently made *a choice* amid complete existential darkness, when my entire life was turned upside-down, to live life alive and on purpose. It was a time when I had everything most dream of and more: a seemingly perfect, infinitely abundant fairytale life from the outside looking in. On the inside, though, numbness, confusion, and disconnection gradually suffocated my spirit because I had forgotten who I was, why I came here, and what I need to live in accordance with my soul. It wasn't an easy choice to make because it ultimately entailed *befriending my body*, with all its aches and pains and perceived flaws and imperfections, with its fears and traumas that colored my experience of reality. To do this, I needed to travel back to a near-death experience from when I was four years old and meet the parts of myself that did not want to return back to life. Parts of myself that would rather stay in the blissful, eternally loving embrace of grace that I was blessed with as my consciousness left my body in the pool house where I almost drowned. As I felt my lungs fill with water, I recall the deliberate sense of surrender that washed over me, a sweet relief from the struggle to reach the surface. Little did I know, this act of surrender was in many ways the very medicine to the aching confusion I felt about being in a body. Little did I know, the ocean of light and embrace of grace I was immersed in when on "the other side" could be infused in every cell of my body, for a sense of belonging here, now. Little did I know, once I did so, the wilderness of my inner knowing would became clear as a starry night sky. And little did I know, because I have experienced both worlds, part of my purpose was to bridge them for myself and others. To invite the gift of this communion, that inner felt-sense-knowing, which connects, transcends, and nourishes our humanity.

> *"Hell served me well, it danced me*
> *straight into the heart of Heaven."*
> ~ Angelica Jill Grace

Not all of you will have experienced a near-death experience (NDE) in which you have had to recollect fragmented pieces of your souls to realize your brilliance, but all of us carry deep-seated wounds and traumas from previous life experiences by default of being human in a world of polarity. This wounding and trauma to a certain extent has a hold on how we live our lives, determining how much love we let in and out and in turn affecting the quality of our relationships. One thing has become very clear to me in my own self-exploration and in therapeutic work with others over the years: to become the vital, healthy, and embodied *bridge-builders of the wild* we were destined to be, it is imperative that we learn how to get out of our heads and into our bodies so that we may retrieve the gifts embedded in the trauma we carry. *Creating a somatic sense of safety is a crucial first step.* This is why I invite you to participate in an exercise where you will connect with your Own Inner

Sanctuary. Your own inner sanctuary is a resource that connects you to your inner power, a place where you feel completely safe, held, unconditionally loved, protected, cared for, and fully accepted for who you are. The more you visit this place in the beginning of your journey, the more resilient your nervous system will become, for it will now have a place to restore and regain strength from the sometimes weary experience of being vulnerably human.

*"You do not have to walk through the desert repenting, you only have to let the soft animal of your body love what it loves . . ."*
~ Mary Oliver, extract from the poem Wild Geese

## Practice: Your Own Inner Sanctuary

Ensure you have a couple of minutes to yourself where you won't be disturbed. Set the space and make yourself comfortable. The cozier the better! Think candles, calming music, essential oils with scents you enjoy, your favourite tea, blankets and pillows. Don't be afraid to go all out on the ambience — the love and attention to these details in the space and the devotional act of preparation sends a message to your body that you and your comfort are important. Once you have settled into your sweet spot, begin by closing your eyes. I now invite you to think of a place in the world where you feel safe and at ease, in joy and contentment, protected and loved. It could be a physical place or a place in the dreaming. A place you have visited or one in the world of fantasy. Become curious about this place. What do you see? What does it look like in this place? Is it inside or outside? What is the temperature? What objects are around your? What colors? Notice a space inside this place to which you feel most drawn. Move toward that space and sit down for a moment. Simply give yourself the gift of being showered with the feelings that this place ignites in you. How exactly does it feel? Peaceful? At home? Like a warm embrace? Safe? Take notice where in your body you feel this way? Bring your hands there and breathe into the feeling. Give yourself permission to be fully present with this feeling and make a point to remember the essence of this place. Before you leave, thank this place for reveal-ing itself to you, for offering itself to be your own inner sanctuary, the place to which you may return whenever it pleases you. Repeat this practice preferably a couple times a day for the next week to reinforce the feelings you awaken here and make this your default destination whenever a situation in life calls for support. Whatever the trigger, your own inner sanctuary is there for your comfort and fulfilment, always.

*"There is more wisdom in your body than in your deepest philosophy."*
~ Friedrich Nietzsche

In addition to this powerful practice, there are *four practical pil-lars* to the process of occupying our body as sacred ground that I decoded through my own psychosomatic explorations.

**Conscious Breathability**

**Intuitive Sounding/Toning**

**Free-flow Movement**

**Sacred Touch**

1.  The breath is one of the most effective and powerful tools for self-regulation. Whether we need to soothe a triggered, stressed, and overwhelmed nervous system or ignite energy in a depleted and underwhelmed body, restoring the body's natural rhythms can be done easily with the conscious act of breathing. Take five deep and slow breaths. In through your nose for focus and calm. Out through your mouth for a sense of grounding and surrender. Notice the cold air around your nostrils as you inhale and the warm air through your mouth as you exhale. Let your mind follow the path of your breath down your throat, your collarbones, your heart and ribcage, your dia-phragm, your belly, and your sex center. Notice how your body spontaneously expands as you inhale and naturally contracts as you exhale. Repeat this as you wake up in the morning, around

lunch time, and as you go to bed at night, as well as whenever you need to de-stress, regain focus, or re-energize.

The motion of expansion and contraction within the cycle of a breath exists everywhere in Nature and beyond and is the very manifestation of what is wild and ever-evolving. Invite curiosity around this constant flow that is part of who you are as a living organism. *Ah, how interesting, I am feeling stressed, or infuriated, or fearful, or stagnant and numb right now! How can I allow myself to feel whatever is here to be felt while staying with myself, not losing myself?* Conscious breathing is one such way! We can gently, in a non-invasive and relaxed way, direct the breath to wherever in the body we experience contracting and soften into it.

2.    Another is a form of expression that has the power to liberate tensions in the body and connect us to an embodied confidence and celebration of who we are is *Intuitive Sounding/Toning*. You may feel weird and awkward if this is your first time playing with your voice in this way (especially if you, like me, were raised to be a people-pleasing "good girl", bound by shackles of shame and deep down fearing to take space and be "too much"). Don't let that turn you off! Stick with the practice, I double dare you, and it will become one of your beloved go-to's for enchanting your wild femme nature out to play. But don't take my word for it . . . Closing your eyes if this feels comfortable to you, simply begin to notice your heart. Recognize that you have a heart. A heart that is pumping blood into all your veins throughout your entire body. A heart that is working non-stop, diligently, to keep you alive. Notice if you can feel your heart beating and connect to any feeling or sensation that resides here, right now. If you are unfamiliar with this kind of mind-body connection, it may take a while before you begin to feel something arise; this is to be expected. Have patience and stay with the practice, bringing yourself back to the heart whenever your mind wanders. As

you become aware of a feeling or sensation in this body part, ask yourself how this emotion or felt sense would sound if it had a sound? Let this sound come from the core of the sensation and give yourself to the sound. Do not worry about how it sounds; this is an opportunity to liberate your voice and express without agenda. No one to impress, nothing to perform. Simply sound. It could sound like "AaaaAAAaah" or "OoOooo" or "AaaaaEeeeelilihheeeOoOoAaaa." Anything and everything is wonderful as long as it is a sound coming through you — even if to you it sounds like just noise! Your focus is on the feeling in your body as you sound. Do this for a couple minutes or however long it pleases you. As you return to silence, notice the vibrations still lingering in your body from your own sound and anything else arising in the wake of your expression. (Pssst, this practice works even greater wonders in the company of trusted sisters! Harmonize away!)

*"Sensuality is how we make sense of reality."*
~ Dr. Saida Desiléts

3.   The third practice, *Free-flow Movement*, can assist us in getting our issues out of our tissues and invite in whatever quality, emotion, or state of mind we wish to experience. These bodies of ours are adaptive by nature and capable of the most incredible expressions as true works of art. Most of us, however, are not tapping in to this inherent potential in our everyday lives but instead choose to neglect our bodies by either sitting still too much or forcing our bodies by over-exercising. This mini-exercise works both with music or without. If you wish, put on one of your favourite tunes. To connect with your body's natural rhythm and let it move you, close your eyes and bring your attention inward. Feel your feet touch the ground and the support from the ground beneath you. Notice your breath and begin to invite a movement from within your body that feels good to you right now. Notice what pace of movement feels good and give yourself to the motion. How

would your inner wild woman move? Let her out. All of her. Lose yourself in the movement and if you have music on, let the sound penetrate your cells. Invite a sense of wonder for this form and the bio-intelligence that is pulsing within it.

4.    The fourth practical pillar of reconnecting with our body, activating our somatic genius, and embodying our wild wisdom is *Sacred Touch*. This is a sensually invigorating, compassionately loving way of becoming our body's best friend, nurturer, and sacred lover. A highly effective way of soothing the body whenever it needs calming down or igniting a sense of relaxed arousal to embrace our sensual, sexual nature as women of fierce, feminine power. Sit or lie down comfortably. Close your eyes and notice your breath. Take three deep and slow breaths into your heart, letting the nourishment of breath make love to your insides. Take another three deep breaths into your lower belly. How can you soften to receive the sweet sensation of breath as though it is your most treasured lover moving into you as a gentle wave of abandoned lust? Place your hands now on top of your belly. Notice what it feels like for your belly to be held here in the palm of your hands. If you are inspired to start moving your hands, exploring your body at your own pace, rhythm, and pressure, please do so. If you feel the need to simply stay here in stillness, receiving the comfort of your own touch deeper and deeper, you are free to do so. This exercise is for your own pleasure. This moment of exploring what feels good to your body is the greatest gift you could give yourself. Once you are one with what your body desires, you shall move as the wildly embodied, mystical creature of bridge-building power that you are. The Earth will quake in your honor as you sway, howl, growl, and whatever else is authentically expressed through you for the liberation of all children, women, and men who are suppressing their true nature.

May these practices offer you all the support you crave for the openings you desire. Whatever battles you are fighting in life right now, know that you are always one breath, sound, movement, and touch away from connecting with the grace that holds you and the embodied wisdom of the wilderness that you are.

Breathing, singing, dancing, and savoring my sensuality beside you.

# SHE IS FLUID

# WITH HER

# FEELINGS.

She is "wild" because she keeps her own last name.

She is "wild" because she will drink and dance the night away.

She is "wild" because she curses.

She is "wild" for not conforming to a 9-5.

She is "wild" for taking risks instead of playing safe.

She is "wild" because she stands up against injustice.

She is "wild" because she speaks her mind.

She is "wild" because she is self-reliant.

She is wild because she knows it is her only way to be.

~ Ky-Lee Hanson

---

UNLEASHING HER WILD

# EPILOGUE

Feminine is (not) weak.

Society has influenced us to focus on certain characteristics of the Feminine. We are to be quiet, soft, and calm. "Feminine is weak, Masculine is strong." The Feminine naturally stays within the mind, and Masculine in the physical.

There has been a global imbalance, and the Masculine has been too strong, it has become dominating. A goal that within every person, the Feminine buried, the Masculine putting on a show. We have had to be one or the other in each moment, unable to find balance.

If you feel over extended in your job, if you have been pushing for external success, moving so fast and hot, then your Masculine could be in a greater state. Your Feminine nature needs attention. Take inward time, be one with the night, quiet your environment, and be still.

If you feel isolated, trapped, tired, you may need to pay attention to your Masculine energy as the Feminine is overworked.

When one is greater, unleash the other and find a middle ground where both can flourish and coexist.

Your life is in constant motion. Change is the one certainty you can count on. With this fact, take each moment of balance as they come. One week, you may need to focus more attention on your feminine side, the next week the masculine. Each task you face requires a different tool; think of balancing energies from the same perspective.[1]

**How can you tap into each energy?** Some practices one can explore to heighten each energy could be as follows:

---

1    https://chopra.com/articles/how-to-balance-your-female-and-male-energy

## Feminine: the Feminine is creative and nurturing

- Redecorating a room
- Art
- Making music
- Encourage those around you
- Practice positivity
- Think holistically
- Nurture yourself and others with fresh food, water, and rest
- Touch: Hugs, cuddles, massage, high-fives, and fist bumps
- Rest
- Write

## Masculine: the Masculine energy is active and logical

- Explore science
- Get active in a physical way: gym, lift weights
- Start a new project that has a definitive end (construction)
- Be competitive: sports, games, competition
- Learn something new
- Set new goals
- Converse with others about your goals

The Masculine and Feminine also govern our physical bodies. The Feminine is the left side of the body, where as the Masculine is the right side. If you tend to have injuries on one side of the body, you could be operating from that energy too greatly. When one is over-extended, we need to pay attention to the other to gain a sense of balance.

Take time for you in regard to either energy you might be currently experiencing life from. Each moment in life will affect you, and it is a constant exercise to achieve balance. Have goals but enjoy the journey, be open to change. Apply logic but don't forget about creative expression. Spend time with people that challenge you but also welcome touch and comfort from others. Give but also receive. Be active but sleep well. Speak but also think.

You are many. You are all. You are whole.

UNLEASHING HER WILD

WOMAN

INTUITIVE

LONE

DARING

# ACKNOWLEDGMENTS

*To all of the Wild (and not so Wild) Women who have come before me and made it safe to speak my truth. To my teachers and guides, Taketomi, Red Hawk Woman, Wild Rose Woman and the beautiful Angela, thank you for always loving me in all my incarnations and encouraging my growth and lighting my path. I am the woman I am today because of the women that you all are. I hold my hands up to you. Finally, to my half-side, Christopher, who has been my greatest champion. You have allowed me the space to become the best woman I have ever been. You allow me always to blossom and shine and be "big" without ever diminishing or dinning my light. You are my Wolf, my Warrior and my greatest blessing. You have kept the fire, chopped the wood and carried the water for me on our Red Road and I am so thankful for that. I am better because of you. I love you with my whole heart.*
\- Donna Tack

*To my mother, who is everything I ever needed her to be.*
\- Kiki Carr

*This chapter is dedicated to all women who are doing the deep inner work to heal their pain, their ancestors pain and to leave a better world for their daughters and their daughters daughters. This is how we as a collective will shift mama Gaia into a higher vibration of love. When one of us heals, we all begin to heal.*
\- Eleni Gray

*My eternal gratitude goes out to my Jungian analyst, whose guidance has modeled the ways of the Wild Woman and Wise Elder, in ways I have yet to fully unravel. I am grateful for the love and support of my family, Nancy Lyddane, George Lyddane, and Chris Lyddane, who serve as my foundation.*
\- Mollie Lyddane

*Thank you beyond Thank Yous to my parents, who have sup-ported me in everything, in every way. To my boyfriend who has stood by me, and for me, when my life so completely changed halfway through, and who still loves me "in the weird." To my Woo Crew for really "getting me." To my ride-or-die, Griffin, guard cat and Cosmic travel buddy. To my clients for trusting me that you truly ARE meant for more. And to those I call my Cosmic Team — for your blessings, your guidance, your teachings, your tough love, your patience, and your guardianship. In Love, Light, and Truth, always.*
- Healther Allison

*As always, my heart is bound to those who love my mind, and my mind is bound to those who know my heart. If you're won-dering if that's you, it probably is. I am grateful for the chance to get thoughts out, this time in a collection, with all the amazing other souls, who are a part of this Wild project- -and not just in the post-it notes I usually accumulate into scrap notebooks. My capacity for literal literary litter is astounding.*
*AB - you pushed me to write. Write anything. Write young.*
*Don't wait . . .*
*. . . I didn't.*
- S.C. Vollmer

*I want to acknowledge the wilderness in all the women who came before us and in those who are yet to come. I also want to honour my beloved Mother, Inger Lundberg. Thank you for giving me life, reminding me of my potential and unwaveringly being by my side.*
- Angelica Jill Grace

THIS IS THE

WILD.

UNLEASHING HER WILD

# GOLDEN BRICK ROAD
**PUBLISHING HOUSE**

Link arms with us as we pave new paths to a better and more expansive world.

Golden Brick Road Publishing House (GBRPH) is a small, independently initiated boutique press created to provide social-innovation entrepreneurs, experts, and leaders a space in which they can develop their writing skills and content to reach existing audiences as well as new readers.

Serving an ambitious catalogue of books by individual authors, GBRPH also boasts a unique co-author program that capitalizes on the concept of "many hands make light work." GBRPH works with our authors as partners. Thanks to the value, originality, and fresh ideas we provide our readers, GBRPH books are now available in bookstores across North America.

We aim to develop content that effects positive social change while empowering and educating our members to help them strengthen themselves and the services they provide to their clients.

Iconoclastic, ambitious, and set to enable social innovation, GBRPH is helping our writers/partners make cultural change one book at a time.

Inquire today at www.goldenbrickroad.pub

Connect with our authors and readers at GBRSociety.com

UNLEASH

YOUR

WILD.

UNLEASHING HER WILD

Made in the USA
Columbia, SC
12 November 2019

83115227R00093